"This book is exceptionally well-written and replete with original and thought-provoking ideas to reflect upon and consider. Dr. Miller's writing has been informed by his wealth of knowledge across multiple disciplines, his many years as a therapist, and his genuine compassion. He makes what may be considered esoteric, very accessible. For anyone interested in probing deeper into the areas of media, ritual, and making meaning in these times, I enthusiastically recommend this book."

—ALAN FORREST,
Professor, Department of Counselor Education,
Radford University

In these pages, Chris Miller brings an intellectual agility and extensive knowledge of philosophical and psychoanalytical theory to provide a fascinating study of what he terms fusion: the conscious and unconscious processes by which people's subjectivities are "influenced heavily, violated, and ultimately stolen by experience with media." *Pixilated Practices* is at times controversial and often brilliant in its analysis of the ways that media in the 21$^{st}$century have infiltrated the fabric of human subjectivity. It is, ultimately, a cautionary tale infused with poetic prescription.

—DIANE RICHARD-ALLERDYCE, PH.D.,
Chair & Faculty, Humanities & Culture Ph.D. Program
in Interdisciplinary Studies, Union Institute & University

# Pixilated Practices

# Pixilated Practices

## Media, Ritual, and Identity

CHRISTOPHER PEYTON MILLER

WIPF & STOCK · Eugene, Oregon

PIXILATED PRACTICES
Media, Ritual, and Identity

Wipf & Stock
An Imprint of Wipf and Stock Publishers
199 W. 8th Ave., Suite 3
Eugene, OR 97401

www.wipfandstock.com

PAPERBACK ISBN: 978-1-7252-6022-1
HARDCOVER ISBN: 978-1-7252-6021-4
EBOOK ISBN: 978-1-7252-6023-8

Manufactured in the U.S.A.   07/06/20

*I am dedicating this book to my wife Kathy
who has been beside me in all matters
and is a beacon of light to the world.*

# Contents

# Preface

FUSION IS THE PHENOMENON whereby persons are connected to media devices in a way that captivates them and then influences the way in which persons go about thinking and living in the world. The definition of *media* here is broad and includes television, social media, use of the personal computer, use of smart phones, and video-gaming. This work investigates and demonstrates the way participation affects persons. The other phenomenon connected to fusion, the subject-media process, which is the mechanism whereby the masses are affected by these media and the representations they promote, greatly influences the masses because people follow the information and images in a way that is quite concerning. *The premise here is that media have come to replace ritual life and the meaning ritual provides.*

In this book, *media* is defined and specified as all visual and auditory representations, especially on screens or monitors. What is not meant here is "the mainstream media," nor ideological notions such as "leftist" or "the Right." The field of media studies has been aware of the ritualistic way in which individuals use media for some time now. Karin Becker has the understanding of ritual events as "spontaneous performances."[1] Becker goes on to state rituals "deconstruct a dominant social hierarchy and its values."[2] The essential function and process of the subject-media process is to create meaning and sustain it in such a way as to move the

1. Becker, "Media and the Ritual Process," 629.
2. Becker, "Media and the Ritual Process," 629.

masses through a global reorientation or paradigm shift. This de-construction does not lead to social justice but has no particular aim other than to propel the agendas of the hegemonic forces of the time. It is not obvious there is any justice done necessarily by the media ritual process; it tends to be interested in promoting the consumption of further media. This does not exclude the use of media to promote agendas, though this can certainly happen. It should also be noted that media can be used for control and pro-paganda. Becker also states that "conceptualizing ritual as *cultural performance* can clarify how media are used in the construction of meaning."[3] Fusion and the subject-media process are not directive intentional phenomena; therefore, the notion of media as Becker indicates, creating a "public event's significance as an *inclusive* cul-tural performance" is not in the purview of what media ritual does in society in the postmodern cyberspace age.[4]

Nick Couldry states there are those who argue the use of the term *ritual* flies "in the face of many claims that we live in an age of 'de-traditionalisation'" and that from that position ritual is a part of the "relics of the past."[5] Couldry brings up the relevant point that Maurice Bloch and Pierre Bourdieu raise: ritual has been used for conflict management and for masking inequality.[6] Ritual, Couldry argues, "remains an important term in grasping what media do and how social institutions work."[7] Couldry also proposes that media serve as an organizational function and offer connectivity for mem-bers of society. There is the matter of social cohesion, which fusion only provides on the virtual level; this is a questionable assumption, given the nature of virtual relationships. Biswarup Sen suggests that through information reciprocating there is a certain "'thing-like' aspect of information" which "enables it to function as a ritualistic tool that helps shape our selves."[8] Sen discusses the relationship

3. Becker, "Media and the Ritual Process," 630 (emphasis original).
4. Becker, "Media and the Ritual Process," 639 (emphasis original).
5. Couldry, "Media Rituals," 60.
6. Couldry, "Media Rituals," 61.
7. Couldry, "Media Rituals," 61.
8. Sen, "Information as Ritual," 1.

between the online and offline self, stating: "information as ritual does for the contemporary self what communication as ritual does for society."[9]

Sen alliterates the way in which the "online self" attempts to substantiate themselves in the virtual world when he writes about the "self" that "ceaselessly manufactures subjective bits to disseminate them along the objective, informational grid of the network."[10] Sen is missing what fusion demonstrates well. In fusion, the subject and object, or the virtual and the actual, or any other dialectical experience, is dissolved as the univocal speaks for the process and the person becomes one with the media process. What remains missing in the exploration of ritual in media studies is the resolution of dialectical thinking. The recognition of the one in lieu of the dual is critical in understanding how the person or subject experiences only the process and is one within fusion.

In a discussion of ritual, Zali Gurevitch and Gideon Aran state that Mircea Eliade, a famous historian of religion, "relates the notion of the Other to the establishment of man as man-at-home in the world. He highlights place as phenomenon of return where the movement is always from chaos to cosmos, from the dispersed to the centered, from non-place to place."[11] Another understanding is that of the sociopsychological perspective, which takes into account the relationality of ritual participants. An example of the way participation in ritual affects each individual is found in a study of synchronous arousal, which is related to empathy and affective mirroring. When studying fire-walkers and the coupling of experience and socially modulated affects, Ivana Konvalinka, et al., demonstrate "the synchrony of the physiological markers shared by the two beings (both fire-walkers and onlooker) cannot be due to direct exchange of matter or energy, leaving only the information available to spectators and participants as the basis of the coupling."[12]

9. Sen, "Information as Ritual," 2.

10. Sen, "Information as Ritual," 7.

11. Gurevitch and Aran, "Never in Place," 136.

12. Konvalinka, et al., "Synchronized Arousal," 8518.

For the spectators of the ritual there is a physiological synchrony, which happens in the observation.

Pascal Boyer and Pierre Liénard express the following judgment on the matter of social investment in ritual and the cost of such as follows: "It is a cognitive and evolutionary puzzle that humans perform rituals, given the waste of time and resources involved."[13] This critical approach is far removed from the religious and philosophical speculation of Mircea Eliade. What can be learned from scholarship about ritual, from religion, psychology, philosophy, social psychology, and anthropology seems certain to construe ritual in many different ways. However, it seems participation in ritual is powerful on an individual and a group level, regardless of one's disciplinary orientation. What the process of ritual reveals about media involvement is significant. Dru Johnson points to the performative nature of who and what persons are when he states: "Some of us wait until life has broken down before examining our ritualed world. But others of us want to understand our rituals now. When we do, we discover ways to foster and sustain good ritualed lives, lives aimed at discernment and flourishing."[14] In the spirit of this understanding, what is sought to be made known is that ritual is something that has been stolen by media, and so too identity is robbed of the person and the masses by media.

Media have become such a large part of our lives; indeed, they have become our lives. Some examples of the ways Christians are fused to or embedded in media are as follows.

Churches spend thousands of dollars on digital signs to attract the public to church events. Screens (television monitors) have become commonplace in churches, from their prayer chapels to their worship areas. Churches invest in expensive websites; Sunday school classes critique movies; and youth group members post their selfies on Instagram. Christians worship via the screen, vicariously feeding on the content they view. But through the subject-media process, ritual is divested of its power and transformed into media. According to James K. A. Smith, people "work with some

13. Boyer and Liénard, "Why Ritualized Behavior?," 612.
14. Johnson, *Human Rites*, 2.

fundamental (though unstated) assumptions about what sorts of creatures (they) are—and therefore what sorts of learners (they) are."[15] Christians have assumptions about who they are, but these assumptions get shifted by the identificatory powers of media participation. It is notable that God did not want the people of Israel to participate in the rituals and idolatry of other people groups, because God desired that the Israelites be identified as God's own. Persons are transformed by God's rituals, but now they are constructed by media representations. The children of Israel participated in the ritual of worshiping the golden calf, crafted by their own hands, at the foot of Mt. Sinai. This ritual, which Israel participated in, was sacrilege, disgusting in both the eyes of the Lord and Moses. Participating in the multitude of media rituals could be understood as a similar case of idolatry because of the interest in images on a screen and their power over the subject. The fusion process is a violation by the media process, of which persons fall victim. Idolatry, particularly "I"conography, is a manifestation of fusion. The church is to be defined by its communion with God, but this is not happening when media presentation is at the fore. Participation in media through the power media hve informs one's identity. Johnson points out that "Rites always have an invisible arrow through them, pointing toward something else. They dispose us to see something being shown to us, both past and present."[16] The invisible target of media ritual is the church member themselves; unfortunately, being conscious of this is not enough to facilitate one's escape from the grip of fusion, as we shall see.

15. Smith, *You Are What You Love*, 2.

16. Johnson, *Human Rites*, 59.

# 1

# Ritual and Meaning in a Cyberworld

SO YOU WALK INTO *a restaurant and there it is on the wall. In an attempt to avoid it, you turn toward another wall. There it is again, a device similar to what you have been looking at this morning. Your connection to the world is inevitable; whether you want it or not, it is there. It is not Big Brother, you surmise, because, as you tell yourself, "it does not control me." A woman in a lavender-and-white-flower blouse catches your attention. "There she is again. I just saw her this morning. It's Kelly." The people you love the most are on the air. Let's face it, you have a choice: either look at the screen or look at the screen. Eyes are trained to follow the pixels.*

*People like Kelly are so much a part of our lives that they certainly go by their first names. She is more than an acquaintance, and she is with you every morning of the week. We understand who we are in relationship to whom and what we see on the screen. "Sitting in the corner of the restaurant is not enough, if I even wanted to escape her, which I don't want to do."*

There is a process that has proven over many centuries to dissolve the self. It is known as ritual. Just as individuals are divested of social imprints and reinvested with new meanings through ritual, they too are divested of psychological character and the soul is reinvented in the ritual space. Interestingly enough, a connection emerges between media usage and ritual. Looking at how

1

ritual affects us helps us recognize how meaning is constructed and personhood is instantiated. Ritual has determined the life of many peoples, and media have a similar effect. *Today media devices fulfill for us the role that ritual has for many thousands of years.* There are various philosophical, psychological, psychosocial, and ethical implications in the way individuals interact with media devices, even as they unwittingly participate. The deepest part of our being is touched by ritual; our souls are caught in that space where meaning is made. Meaning is made in and through media, just as it is in ritual.

Ritual serves as the source of meaning-making, helps us understand our world, and has served to order our world despite all its complexities. The deepest part of ourselves is touched by ritual, which gives us significance. The term *ritual* may carry, for many, connotations of archaic religious life and ways of coping with the world. These mechanisms of coping may seem out of step with modern ways of approaching life. Nonetheless, little does anyone realize that media are doing the same thing in modern and postmodern times. Social changes are reined in by meaning, and meaning is constructed by ritual. No matter how much a person envisions themselves as an independent individual, their meaning is constructed socially. Just as Westerners conceive of the East to be "oriental," likewise we perceive ourselves as not in need of ritual. It should come as no surprise that we abhor being told that meaning is constructed outside of ourselves, by powers larger than ourselves, through cultural changes. Each person likes to believe, in a free society, that "I make my own meaning." Social scientists and theorists have noted the phenomenon of social meaning construction. Lives are directed by representations and media, as Stuart Hall has suggested. I suggest something else is going on between ourselves and media which has less to do with content (like representation) and more to do with process.

However, before venturing into how media in today's world shape our souls, a closer look at media is warranted. Earlier forms of media include theatrical performance, dance, songs, and storytelling. The underpinning of these was *ritual*: acts of meaning-making within the context of a community. Ritual had carried the meaning of life, with all of its complexity, throughout the lives of communities. The content of what persons know by way of communicating meaning through ritual is years of wisdom and knowledge about embodied life. Many civilizations have developed and passed, and they have made their imprint on the story of this world. It seems fusion (as I call the process of ritualizing, which comes with our experiences of media) is quickly replacing the usual nature by which persons store information. There is a newer organizing principle. It seems as though bytes and flashes of information on screens are stored in digital spaces within the mind. Through fusion, the person practices the media moment, just as one might practice a ritual. That there is a place where meaning is constructed is evidenced by how persons engage with an other outside themselves. That other is the media device, which brings the person pleasure at the cost of their individuality. Media devices create a comfortable life for us; they give us the ability to accomplish tasks that used to be time-consuming and difficult.

Ritual forms and mores have been shaped by audiovisual media for decades now. The phenomena of globalization, and the digital collections of memories, are now the common means of experiencing life. Hence, these epiphenomena of the process between the subject and media now carry the memes of the newest global civilization. Globalization, which has grown as fast as the internet, has pressured us with the illusion of many more choices in terms of self-definition. Thus, globalization has put our allegiance in the hands of those who create the ideal self through media. Through this creating process, meaning is constructed.

Emile Durkheim explained that representations are powerful and work within meaning-making. Meaning is visceral and affective, touching the heart and developing deep within us. Myth is part of the role of media, one myth upstaging the next as time passes. Only obscenity is what becomes great in our day. It is almost always short-lived, and then it is lost in obscurity. This is an estimation of how media work *in* our present world, or rather, *as* our present world. Mores have been shaped by media of all sorts. In this work, I will explain there *is a process*, which is as powerful as the ritual of ancient times. This process infuses persons with meaning that has the ability to disturb, subvert, and construct images and actions which have demonstrable effects on the very nature of our being. From temple to reality television, the masses have collected an ethos from the experiences and images that have been presented to them.

Ritual within cultic life has a body inscribed with markings that have far-reaching implications for the follower's eternal destiny. In its traditional sense, ritual has the power to determine what the participant believes about the existence of a world beyond. This type of meaning construction is what persons have always lusted to participate in: to be in process with the transpersonal. Persons that exist within these rituals learn there is something meaningful outside, but inclusive of, the body. The meaning-making process lies in, ahead of, and beyond our present reality. Ritual is conjoined with media in the postmodern world in such a way as to fuse a person or population to a meaning-making apparatus known as the screen. No matter the size of the screen, the world hangs in the balance of this process called fusion.

Fusion is the singular event process whereby a person loses their identity in media; this entrapment is a violation of one's will and personal efficacy. Fusion happens very early in the life of the individual as they are exposed to media. It is a reality that one is born into media, and remains immersed in it most of the hours in the day and night. Fusion is inescapable for the person who lives in the postmodern world. Psychological territories are impacted by both process and content between the body and media. In fusion, the process of media is more influential than content, when one pursues the investigation of media and representations of the body.

Meaning-making is a commercial activity about something that is deeper within, involving every aspect of our lives. Indeed, the person is robbed of metaphysical meanings and made subject to violation by media. The soul is emptied of its traditional meaning and given a meaning that befits the nature of our digital world. A close look at media demonstrates where the body is designed. The reaction between the corporeal body's territory and that of the imposing unnatural body of media causes a disarray of the person's conceptualization of the body. The investigation of the process of fusion, and the overwriting of the body through media rituals, are what I intend to examine in this book. In this pursuit it will become apparent media are replacing ritual in the battle for the physical and psychological territories of the person. The fusion process involves a symbolic *process* that becomes increasingly vast with each passing day, gaining influence over the person more strongly than ever. The insurmountable influx of body representations from media is often too much for the person to digest.

The philosophical psychoanalytic position of Jacques Lacan on the subject of experience as it resides within conscious and unconscious space is of considerable relevance to the understanding of how the individual person experiences ritual and media. The fusion process, or media enmeshment of the person, is best understood through the Lacanian lens. The individual demonstrates weakness, or alienation, through the subject, and becomes vulnerable to inescapable engagement with media. Because there is no escape from this process between media and the subject, which is more than just the constant presence of media, the subject becomes dissolved in media and the media process. The dissolving subject is linked to media ritual and the loss of the ability to experience real ritual life. The thread that runs through Lacan's theory is that the subject is split between the conscious and unconscious worlds within the person. *This split leads to the alienation which then opens the way for media to infiltrate and violate the boundaries of the person.*

The subjective experience of a person is that which exists as a psychologically oriented phenomenon or a philosophical entity which is susceptible to being violated by something which is external to the subject. Media have the power to overwhelm the subject and envelop it in media's ways and states of being. One is compelled to relax and enjoy, or join and utilize media to reach certain attainable emotional and cognitive states. That which is actually happening is a seduction by media to draw in the subject coercively into relationship with media's content and process. The violation happens through a subtle hidden process. The entangling effect of media in relation to the subject is tantamount to abuse of the person's efficacy. The person finds themselves in a situation where there is a fixed power relationship. One does not get a say in their experience, but experiences the illusion of choice and is therefore manipulated by media. This entrapment of the individual is like reaching the point of loss of control in an intense ritual. The subject is fascinated and seduced by the flash and frenzy of stimuli that media produce. Extra pixelation and brush-ups invite the person into media, and enticing scenarios engage the subject at its weakest point: the level of alienation it experiences.

Because the subject is split and therefore susceptible to endorsement of unwanted content and process, media bombardment cannot be resisted. There is a sort of violation of the subject that overpowers and is the very fusion one cannot resist. The person is like a fish in water, unable to see what is happening or understand they are constantly embedded in media. Thinking, as an experience of television and internet, has continuously exposed the person to the same content with the same messages. Persons have succeeded in pushing aside the imagination in favor of manipulation.

Jacques Lacan once stated the unconscious is structured like a language; in the twenty-first century, the structure has been reduced to visual and auditory processes. Bodily experience is set aside by the influence of media. The structure of the conscious and unconscious is becoming like a screen with multiple visual and auditory interventions by media to force one to alter their consciousness in favor of the imagery and energy of the process of fusion. Slavoj Žižek discusses "symbolic fictions" in relationship to media and the concept of self-identity, questioning the presence of an agenda within media that causes persons to define themselves in a certain manner. The problem is, agenda aside, persons do reflect on self-definition and identity in relation to their involvement in media. Whether one dabbles in self-defining within social media spaces or identifies with and models themselves after a television personality, the action of media plays into one's performance of self in the world as they know it. The world as it is known is, in fact, media itself.

There is a collective, which is the subject-media process, and it proffers the many persons affected by fusion into one body. This collective happens when media take over the bodily experience of all persons. This is termed "the body of media." All persons could be considered one in that media make meaning that is consistent and equivalent for all, and create a common worldview for all to share. The body of media is the conglomerate of subjects that are enveloped by fusion. The subject-media process is the force of the media process delivered to the masses.

The subject-media process happens on a large scale, whereby the masses are subject to a process that engulfs them in a worldview and narrative that is media-driven, often providing the same narrative for everyone; this is where the body of media comes into play. The body of media is the collective experience of the masses that indicates the enumeration of data that each is exposed to. The body of media has a particular focus on the lived body of the individual: the trend of media and society's representation and expectation of what the body norm is at that particular time in history, which is defined by media as well. History in media representation is always revisionist in the sense that it is evolving within the understanding of each person. It is probable that history is media, because of the all-consuming nature and data representation of media's history at any given time or moment. The history of the body in media has changed over time.

Paul Watzlawick discusses how media have changed as they have shifted away from literature. Watzlawick explains there was a "time when naïve storytelling, when the construction of well-made plays, when trust in the instrument of language altogether had become problematic."[1] Watzlawick also spoke of how "trust in the old forms (of communicating meaning), trust in the relationship with the public had vanished . . . loss of confidence on the part of the artist, and (there was) the advent of the new media film and television."[2] There was suddenly an invasion of stimuli as no one had seen before. This invasion was the accomplice of the subject-media process; static media was left in the wake of technology.

Once one is doused in media, as though the masses are not already like fish in water, then the question becomes: Is there a control factor or a Big Brother? There is no concrete measureable data that proves such a theory, but media are fashionable, inviting, valued ways to go about decision-making in life. The seeming multiplicity

1. Watzlawick, *Invented Reality,* 166.
2. Watzlawick, *Invented Reality,* 166.

of choices and options determine, in large part, our culture and its multiculturalism. Although there seem to be many choices, there is the fusion effect of the univocal; persons do not have as much choice as it would seem.

There is the limitation of the univocal because it offers no choice. Though it would seem media offer many choices, there is the univocity of media experience. The subject is challenged by the explicit use and unambiguous nature of what one understands, which is flatness. Fusion offers no choice disguised as choice. Media are supra-existent, beyond simple or complex understandings of existence; media exist prior to thinking in any category. One is born into media, just as Lacan would say one is born into language. Instead of ritual, which is largely influential in a deterministic way, media have taken on the role of being deterministic, while pretending to offer choice.

Fusion is a tailored experience for the individual, just as the subject-media process is for the masses, whereby the person becomes lost in media and loses their identity in the process. The subject-media process can explain why so many are fused to the screen and experience one and the same illusion of reality, which leads well into explaining fusion as the individual loss of ritual and self. Since fusion is a process between media and subject, often it will stand alone as an individual demarcation between the real world and the virtual world. The demarcation, however, becomes less clear as the person enters fusion. The line between the subject and media becomes increasingly thin as the fusion process envelops the subject and the person becomes the process itself. There comes a point of blurring and then disappearance of any delineation between person and media. The process of fusion replaces the need for ritual life in the postmodern world. The screen takes the place of the person's need for ritual and meaning-making, drying up the need for the personal experience of relationship and communion with other people.

This work will primarily focus on subject and experience, fusion, subject-media process, identity, relationship, gaming/virtual reality, and other matters directly related to media representations. This work always takes seriously the manner in which media violate them the subjective experience of those exposed to them. Through this work, one will come to understand how persons born in the postmodern era, and even before, are swimming in media; the conscious and the unconscious are structured as media are structured. It is a post-truth world, and at this time in history, media are creating the very nature of experience that was once occupied by ritual. Media have replaced the meaning-making nature of life, especially as it has been in previous times expounded by ritual. The person no longer transcends, becomes authentic, or self-actualizes in relation to reality, because media *is* reality. Media control experience, violate, and manipulate with their narrative in such a way as to pain the individual psychically and physically. Media have taken on the role of ritual and invaded the life and worldview of the masses.

# 2

# Language and Meaning

*Sitting in the grass and the leaves, noticing the brown, orange, red, and green around you, you are enjoying nature while taking in philosophy from your textbook, which states that "A subject is an observer and an object is a thing observed." So you begin to wonder what it is to be an observer, just for a moment slipping into a kind of trance state as you look upon the fall colors. An observer of the object—the leaf, tree bark, light blue sky, and brilliant sunlight—is what you are, and these shape the way you think and feel. It becomes apparent to you that reality is not somewhere other than where you are in nature, or closed off in your room where you see all four walls and notice the angles in each corner of your room. In your room, though, is the ultimate subject experience, that of the interaction you have with your gaming console. You "allow" yourself to go headlong into a "subject position" through which you notice the object of your desire (the ideal object). So where is your real subjective world? Is it out in the fall? Is it being the subject in a reality you do not even have tangible truth about and of which you have no connection with your senses? The primal nature of the subject of your experience has been shunted or pushed away from its real experience as the "I" that you are really about. There is a decay you feel about your subject, yet you continue to play the games. The same goes for the movies you get absorbed in and your favorite television shows. There is a connection between you and your objective world even though you cannot touch or feel it. A sparrow flutters by and you are startled out of your daydreaming and wondering. There you sit, in the grass and leaves.*

Subjectivity is the internal state of being through which assertions are made about real experiences of causation which can be exerted via the sense of self. Subjectivity involves the person's tastes, agency, efficacy, and their conscious and unconscious worlds. Subjectivity is the presentation of oneself to oneself and to the world as conceived by the individual and the audience; it is a sharing of something that is experienced as firm and not changing and yet it is flexible and fluid. This subjectivity, a psychological state synchronous with the external world, is a persistent understanding one must produce in order to be taken as a serious part of others' worlds as well. In Western thought, the subject has been understood over and against the object, and the subject has had primacy in this relationship. In the twentieth century, the nature of the subject came into question with the advent of deconstructionism through the work of Jacques Derrida on Martin Heidegger. I refer to the subject as fragile and not necessarily having primacy over the object. This understanding of subjectivity and the subject is foundational to the development of fusion as the way media act upon the subject.

The work of Lacan lends perspective about subjective experience to the development of the interaction between the individual and media. Lacan does not identify subjectivity as an active process, but as rather an impersonal and passive one. Such a way of thinking enhances the notion of fusion as subjugating the subject and makes it clear the subject is split between the conscious and the unconscious part of the person's experience. Lacan says, "The subject cannot simply be identified with the speaker or the personal pronoun in a sentence. In French the *ennoncé* is exactly the sentence, but there are many *ennoncés* where there is no index of him who utters the *ennoncé*. When I say 'it rains,' the subject of the enunciation is not part of the sentence."[1] In other words, the subject is the result of language and is implied, even when there is no obvious source of enunciation for it.

1. Lacan, "Of Structure," 2.

Lacan once wrote of the subject in the following way: "I am not a poet, but a poem. A poem that is being written, even if it looks like a subject."[2] Lacan was referring to the way in which our sense of subject exists within a semiotic system, a system of language and symbols. Persons are aware of themselves and express the nature of what they experience in language. Expression of subjective experience is done by language both internally and externally. Some internal experiences seem to be actuated through representations, conceptualization, and can be experienced through language. Lacan is well known for his expression that the unconscious is "structured like a language."[3] It is within the system of language or symbols that the person becomes manifest to themselves and the world around them.

Lacan, in saying his experience is a poem being written, demonstrates his understanding of our experience within what he calls the symbolic order. For the most part, a person understands themselves as constancy and permanently represented to themselves. It is not often a person finds it the case that they are not themselves. However, there are times when one is not oneself, when they feel a sense of things being surreal or not quite real. This may happen when someone has lost a lot of sleep or is experiencing extreme anxiety, or even when one is under the influence of a substance like alcohol. This can occur during human development, when magical thinking happens in childhood. Magical thinking occurs when a child imagines themselves in a fictive world and pretends. The child may come to believe this fictional reality is more important than their relationships in the real world. This kind of not-quite-feeling-to-be-oneself might happen when one is daydreaming. In another case a person may behave in ways that are out of character and wonder why they behaved in such a manner. It is through this propensity that fusion can capture the subject.

Lacan's notion of the mirror stage is important in this context. It is during the mirror stage that infants realize autonomy and self-efficacy. The child looks in the mirror and comes to realize the

---

2. Lacan, *Four Fundamental Concepts*, viii.

3. Lacan, *Four Fundamental Concepts*, 203.

body they see is coordinated at their own volition; this is the formation of the sense of a person being a unified entity with control of
its own body. Two other Lacanian notions that are important to
the understanding of fusion are the symbiotic relationship and the
name of the father. The symbiotic relationship is a period of strong
attachment and identification the infant has with the mother that
exists from birth. The relationship with the mother is interrupted
by the father's "no." At this point, an outside force interferes with
symbiosis.

From the time the father interrupts the symbiotic relationship,
the child comes to understand the world is differentiated from the
child. The symbiotic relationship is challenged and altered. In the
fusion process it is media which function as the name of the father
and interrupt the symbiotic relationship with the mother. The subject goes through the weaning process initiated by the name of the
father, or the author of media narrative, otherwise understood as
the overarching worldview. Weaning happens when the symbiosis
is interrupted: when forces outside the subject push the subject into
the field of media. Fusion is the virtual form of the mirror stage.
Media conduct the formation of efficacy and control. In the fusion
process, though, the name of the father, or name of the father of
media narrative, takes control of the subject. The subject is acted
upon and does not carry a strong sense of efficacy.

The subject is affected by its surroundings and is impression-
able; recall again the loss the infant sustains in the mirror stage. A
major loss in life may affect a person's sense of self, such as when
a child loses a parent or one has the loss of a spouse, potentially
altering personality characteristics and one's feeling of being-
in-this-world. An interesting example is when one experiences a
neurological disorder like Korsakoff's syndrome. Oliver Sacks has
observed this phenomenon, in which a person, if there is any identity within, remembers "nothing more than a few seconds. . .con-
tinually disoriented. Abysses of amnesia continually opened
beneath. . .bridge(d). . .nimbly, by fluent confabulations and fictions
of all kinds."[4] The person with Korsakoff's makes up information

4. Sacks, *Man Who Mistook*, 109.

13

about previous forgotten conversations. These seem to be lies intended to compensate for what was forgotten. Being deprived of a continuous world, the person with Korsakoff's syndrome has problems learning from new experiences and is unable to maintain short-term and long-term memory. The individual sees, and interprets out of some unconscious phantasmagoria, a dream of people and things that are a real world to that person. These fabrics of connectivity show that desire is continually seeking to make meaning. The person seems to have intact social skills and the ability to carry on a conversation, but forgets the conversation only moments later. There is an unconscious in the person's internal world that is so powerful that the Korsakoff's sufferer is able to create a scenario which emulates a real set of circumstances, in order to carry on a relatively linear conversation and an identity for themselves. This demonstration of linearity seems relatively coherent and indicates the ability of the subject to be maintained.

In the first sense, the subject is informed inwardly. In a second sense, the subject is informed externally as well, as has been demonstrated by psychologists and philosophers alike. According to David R. Shumway, Michel Foucault's concept of *gaze* "is itself a major innovation in the development of Foucault's ideas about power, knowledge and the subject."[5] As a phenomenon in its own right, the gaze was a force which singled out the persons of difference and monitored their behavior. A person under observation, the gaze, is treated like an object. The gaze is an idea which Foucault illustrates in his works on the power differentials in society. Foucault demonstrates how the gaze was used to capture and persecute people.

The gaze is used by society at large to identify, follow, and change or discriminate against people whose behavior does not fall into acceptable social norms. In Foucault's estimation, throughout history the gaze followed and often haunted many types of persons, from criminals to Christian catechumens. Being in the gaze of the other is how one existed as a subject. This was the case if one did not fit the societal mold. This would have included the vagabond,

5. Shumway, *Michel Foucault*, 46.

the thief, or the insane. And as science was coming into its own, the observation of science became another form of the gaze.

Since cognitive science can measure and observe the nature of mind and subjectivity, scientists note changes in the minds of those who have disordered thoughts and unusual experiences. There are instances in psychopathology or neuropathology where the person experiences loss of the subject, while feeling and thinking that they exist in the gaze of a perceived other. The Truman syndrome involves the belief or delusion that one's life is staged in a virtual reality or that they are being watched on cameras. Jennifer Peltz reported in her work that "Researchers have begun documenting what they dub the 'Truman syndrome,' a delusion afflicting people who are convinced that their lives are secretly playing out on a reality TV show. Scientists say the disorder underscores the influence pop culture can have on mental conditions."[6]

Peltz's article quotes psychiatrist Dr. Joel Gold with the following question: "Is this just a new twist on an old paranoid or grandiose delusion . . . or is there sort of a perfect storm of the culture we're in, in which fame holds such high value?"[7] Neurological aberrations often, as peculiar and uncanny as they can be, explain bizarre behavior and thoughts. But is the Truman syndrome truly an example of fusion? Does the melding together of media and the subject result in a delusion? The Truman syndrome demonstrates the subject's desire for continuity and meaning. Media have somehow enveloped the individual's experience, in the case of the Truman syndrome, and included it only within itself. This is an astounding invention by the subject, however real it is to the person with the syndrome. The person experiencing the Truman syndrome experiences their world as virtual, but real.

It is helpful to have an understanding of the unconscious in order to determine a Lacanian understanding of the subject. Lacan demonstrates the nature of the subject as split between conscious and unconscious process. This understanding of the subject engages with my work here; one can better understand the action of media's

6. Peltz, "To Some Psychiatric Patients," para. 2.

7. Peltz, "To Some Psychiatric Patients," para. 3.

unmitigated power over the subject, which is process. By the 1960s, Lacan began to dis-include language about the opposition of ego and subject; as Lacanian scholar Paul Verhaeghe indicates, "Instead of the opposition and division between ego and subject, the division and splitting within the subject itself comes to the fore. Instead of the term 'subject,' the expression 'divided subject' appears—that is, divided by language."[8] The subject is inadequate to the task of fending off the process of becoming fused to media. The subject is weak. As Verhaeghe states, "the subject has a mere pre-ontological status, which is again closely linked to the status of the unconscious. The ever divided subject is a fading, a vacillation, without any substantiality."[9] The subject is split and fragile in Lacanian thought.

Silvia Rodriguez, in *A Compendium of Lacanian Terms*, explains it quite clearly: "The Lacanian subject is not the unified subject of knowledge, but the subject as it has emerged in the experience of psychoanalysis: divided, inconsistent, incomplete, punctuated rather than 'full.'"[10] Lacan has said, "The unconscious is . . . a thinking with words, with thoughts that escape your vigilance."[11] Though split between the conscious and the unconscious, it seems entirely plausible that the subject is partly a result of the endeavor of language to iterate what is driven from the unconscious. The subject being split evidences its lack of power and leaves one with a loss of being. Lacan says, "Where is the subject? It is necessary to find the subject as a lost object. More precisely this lost object is the support of the subject and in many cases is a more abject thing than you may care to consider."[12] Lacan recognized the potential for loss in the case of the subject, and I see the potential for loss in the process of interaction with media; the subject loses effect to fusion.

Dylan Evans explains a way in which Lacan uses the notion of the subject, which is relevant here as well. Evans explains

8. Verhaeghe, "Causation and Destitution," 164–65.
9. Verhaeghe, "Causation and Destitution," 165.
10. Rodriguez, "Subject," 193.
11. Lacan, "Seminar of Jacques Lacan," 3.
12. Lacan, "Seminar of Jacques Lacan," 3.

> Lacan establishes a distinction between the subject and the EGO which will remain one of the most fundamental distinctions throughout the rest of his work. Whereas the ego is part of the imaginary order, the subject is part of the symbolic. Thus the subject is not simply equivalent to a conscious sense of agency, which is a mere illusion produced by the ego, but to the unconscious; Lacan's 'subject' is the subject of the unconscious.[13]

Certainly the ways in which media work on the subject could avail such an understanding of the subject as a subject of the unconscious. In the Lacanian subject, fragility comes from its split. Such a weak and split nature predisposes person(s) to entrapment in fusion. The basic platform of the self is shifted in such a way as to alter one's perception; to include it in a media process involves interaction with violence and violation. The person and the device become fused by a process which lies beyond the reach of any intention. One's very instincts are manipulated and the person becomes a perfect specimen for continued media exploitation.

In regards to media and the treatment of the subject as unconscious or split, fusion is a process in which the subject is subjugated and disappears in the frenzy and flash of media. The lack of substantiality in the subject, and it being derived from the unconscious, allows for the manipulation of the subject and predetermines the occurrence of the fusion process. The whole of the fusion process (now holding a negative connotation) comes to light when one grasps how the subject works. Media's ensnaring effects are based on desire and seduction, but the vulnerability of the subject as well. If "I am a poem" is any indication, then the subject is written and thus can be scripted by media as well. The subject's conscious nature, the avid use of media, and the person's willful use of media, perpetuate the process of envelopment of the subject by media.

Considering the unconscious, the split subject, and the subtleties of media process configuration and connectivity, the subject is susceptible. In reality, the subject as unconscious and media as subjugating the essence of life together provide a recipe for fusion. When it is understood that the virtual is "realer than real," as Brian

---

13. Evans, *Introductory Dictionary of Lacanian Psychoanalysis*, 197–98.

Massumi has stated, realizing media's potential devastation to the subject only magnifies its effects. Massumi indicates: "There is a seductive image of contemporary culture circulating today. Our world, Jean Baudrillard tells us, has been launched into hyperspace in a kind of postmodern apocalypse. The airless atmosphere has asphyxiated the referent, leaving us satellites in aimless orbit around an empty center."[14] This vulnerability of the subject, in Massumi's statement "the referent," has seemingly developed in the postmodern era.

14. Massumi, "Realer than Real," 90.

# 3

# Fusion and the Subjugated Self

FUSION IS A PROCESS or event that occurs with regard to the individual and media, by which the person becomes one with media; this process transcends person or subject, via occupation by media. We are losing our souls because of the virtual. The flux of our being is altered by and captured in media; our subjectivities are lost in media. This is more than Baudrillard's symbolic exchange; rather, it is a transformation of the individual being into what is experienced as the process and changing nature of media. This process exists regardless of its content and simply stands as a phenomenon on its own.

The following is an example of virtual reality that is experienced in the fusion process. A virtuality of medium is used to provide the help one needs to experience calmness and serenity.

*Sitting. That's all. Counting breaths. Not driven by any intentionality. There is no drive, no fashion of motivation, no pressure to succeed in altered consciousness. The imagery and vocal tone take me to a placid, calming region of "my" mind. I can separate myself from any external influences and follow the voice which leads me through a beatific terrain, with glistening waterfalls and a shimmering lake. Green pastureland and light blue skies reign above my head. A light mist, originating from some waterfalls, softly sprays in my face. I can arrive at this peace of mind with the encouragement of my iPod, trending podcasts, and YouTube videos in the form of relaxation and meditative spirit. This is my placid, private world in which I dwell. Although others use the same medium, I spend this time alone on the Internet, eliminating my mind's-eye view, because the beauty is provided through my connection with my mouse and screen of my PC.*

This placid experience is neither interior nor exterior, but instead is in a virtual space which incites the mind to connectedness. It is the experience of fusion, whereby the whole of one's self becomes caught up in the process. To this extent, the person becomes one with media in the process. The subject is *identical* to media in this process. Therefore, there is no contradistinction, no dialectical moment, and no interior versus exterior. Such envelopment allows for the feeling of disconnect from the world of force and ideas. In fact, there is entrapment of the subject in the process, whereby the will is integrated with media process. Persons become mere connections inside of media process.

Media are reproduced and melded with the subject in the fusion process. Our subjectivity works as a flow; it is almost not there to begin with, in the sense of a concrete self. In a Lacanian understanding or reading, there is no continuous subsistence or substantiation of the subject. The subject is stolen by media's fluidity; even our imagination is questionable and compromised. Gilles Deleuze states it well when he understands that "nothing is done *by* the imagination. . .the production of an idea by the imagination is only a reproduction of an impression."[1] The degree of vividness that makes sense perception acute is found in the pixels of representation. Within the mind of the individual are also intrusive pixels which make up memory. The reproduction is the subject caught in media process.

Sitting in front of a media device is more than just captivating; there is the loss of self in this process. Memories and minds affected by fusion are in a perpetual process of reimaging, distortion, and violence. The more pixels, the more memory, and then the more lost in the process the subject becomes. There is a great and significant loss of control as well. Pixel value and auditory stimuli

---

1. Deleuze, *Empiricism and Subjectivity*, 94 (emphasis original).

that correspond to the fusion process are so overpowering that the subject must give way; it gains integration with media moment by moment. Whether experienced as degrading or orgasmic, media have had a strong grip on the soul and our collective consciousness, and our collective unconscious, for decades.

This also includes absorbing media values about what it means to be a self in the world. The forces draw the subject into relationship with media; the person ultimately comes to understand themselves as identical to a media characterization based in the seeming myriad options. The options seem multiple, but the limit is one, by concomitant force received by the person. There are multiple images that influence what we become, but we all become one person, we become more alike than we realize. The creative process is stifled by media portrayals of what we should become, which are not fair to many. The experience of fusion determines identity by violating the subject. Fusion sucks us in, no matter what our inclination; it is a violation of the subject. Each time one is engaged with a media device, whether it is television, gaming, or a PC, the subject is violated and ensnared.

From birth, one has no other baggage to bring to an experience than that very meaning-making apparatus of the larger media. Even in a child's infancy, media are so pervasive they affect the formation of the subject. Kathryn C. Montgomery extends the concern that there must be a way to clearly present information to children in order to maintain quality of care for their minds. Montgomery states there is a need for policy and protocol "to help ensure the development of a quality digital media culture for children," and there is more to this discussion than meets the eye. It is evident a particular mindset is expected of children in the "digital or information age."[2] Those who determine the appropriate development of media to address the needs of children should consider content and process. Proceeding with the mores and behaviors media will contribute to these children, the fusion process is particularly powerful in giving structure to children, regardless of the content. Children of this era spend most of their time in cyberspace. Even adults fall prey to the entrapment of media

2. Montgomery, *Generation Digital*, 146.

seduction. The virtually real carries with it the strength to determine the lives of child and adult alike.

The nature of the overarching world understanding is a philosophy which heavily influences the way persons exist in the West. The philosophy is seductive and attractive as it continues to deconstruct, to the extent that there is no logic left or even a world of objectivity. This postmodern philosophy is the turn to the subject; the subject desires and is seduced, and therein we have reached an end of history as we know it. History is no longer relevant because everything becomes refocused toward the subject and their likings. These likings are determined by media, the predecessor of any inclination the person might have, because media literally control this process. As in many games, persons are developing and constructing their own worlds. Two errors must be addressed here: persons only have the materials provided to them by media, and fusion happens to the extent that persons no longer have control or efficacy.

The last crushing blow to dialectic is to have an image that is self-affirming, without contradistinction, and that also is fused into collective consciousness. The logical movement from one side of the dichotomous to the opposite, then to the synthesis, is disintegrated into a single movement; this is a singular event which exists as one process. Meaning-making, then, is not found in a dialectical process, through which an identity could be formed. Meaning and identity formation instead evolve in the virtual space in a singular moment, not through anything other than definitions as they are presented on screens. The person gets identity through the imprint of the other as presented on the screen. The screen offers an ideal other not to emulate, but at once to become. This seems like an occasion for expanding the repertoire of which a person might become, whetting their appetite for the ideal ego, which they wish to gain, but in fact it is a singular moment which violates them.

When subjects are caught in this process, they lose will and control over who and what they are to become; they become the fusion process itself. Therefore, fusion is a process of reducing the power of the subject, indeed overpowering the subject. The existential meaning-making I, which is its own destiny, loses will to fusion or the person becomes a mere connection. Fusion is not just a simple turning to the self as deconstructed, but it is to see the subject disappear in the frenzy and flash of media. The subject becomes *identical* to media in this process. In the case of fusion, oneness is lived in the experience of a subject who is crowded in by meaning-making stimuli. Reality is so full of the virtual that the world as the person experiences it cannot be extracted from that which the subject has become: the fusion process. Daniel Wegner states: "we might purposefully suppress the unwanted thought of an upcoming awkward confrontation with someone, and in order to do this concentrate on a television show."[3] This happens all the time at work, at home, or in public. Media and the subject become one through the trap: fusion. This process engages everyone who is exposed to the audio-visual media of today's landscape. It appears at every turn and leaves us in a life of delusion.

Almost everywhere a person goes, the virtual beckons them to participate in this process. Once the screen is introduced in a public setting, it is taboo to look disdainfully away from it. Persons cannot even watch a ballgame in a stadium without being seduced by a huge screen, large enough for all in the stadium to see, in order to watch the game in all its virtuality. Fusion occurs when spectators concentrate on it as though they cannot see the game without it. Each person is caught up in the fusion process, which disallows the experience of reality. If media is in play with the person, and then the person walks away from it, the virtual still continues to change them and becomes part of their narrative.

Fusion is the process of media joining the process of the self, the soul, our very being. Fusion destroys experiences and makes them part of a process outside of the subject. The subject is enfolded into the process as it loses identity and media takes over its vicissitudes. By way of media, this enfolding of the subject into the fusion process involves fear, love, attraction, and indeed seduction. The enfolding by way of seduction and desire is the mechanics of fusion. While some assert that sometime in the near future, our technological and biological evolution will allow persons to create

---

3. Wegner, *White Bears*, 12.

realities for themselves as they please, it seems more likely this creating of reality is compromised, because fusion dampers one's real senses and replaces them with signals from a virtual reality. It is a virtual world that seduces the subject, that tired decomposition; media connect to desires concerning being and meaning. Desire and seduction within and without the subject are all that are left. The opposing forces within and without no longer have sway over the individual. Fusion is an unnecessary drugging process by which one experiences thought that one would otherwise not be exposed to in the real world. The object, which is media, seduces the subject; it then makes an object of the subject, in a carnival of insidious control. Fusion is as compelling as the thoughts of an obsession. When media come into the equation, the subject just moves into its dance.

The subject-media process is the force by which the masses get influenced in such a way as to flood them with ideology. The world has seen accelerating technology within globalization that has emphasized the subject as object of media for such duration as to practically obliterate the subject. The subject loses itself in the global. In a media-driven, postmodern world Hilary Lawson indicates the "impact of reflexivity is in part due to a critical shift of focus, from the individual subject to the text."[4] Media here is the counterpart of text, for our primary source is media. In the postmodern world, each subject is minimized or erased; this erasure is developed in the philosophical tradition of deconstruction, a tradition that began with Martin Heidegger and was later developed by Jacques Derrida. Derrida states: "the idea of the end of man is then always already prescribed in metaphysics, in the thought of the truth of man. What is difficult to conceive of today is an end of man which is not organized by a dialectic of truth and of negativity."[5]

There is a new way of understanding subjectivity; no longer does the subject sit in direct opposition to the object. Dialectic can be seen in the dichotomies such as God/Satan, good/evil, and sanity/insanity. These have been evaporated; these used to be the

4. Lawson, *Reflexivity*, 10.
5. Derrida, "Ends of Man," 42.

battlegrounds for persons' very beings, both body and soul. This dialectic of the old person has been swallowed up into the process of media, i.e. fusion. Indeed, Baudrillard has said persons lose the grandeur of the individual soul. The subject is reduced to violation. Fusion in action, the highlight of the twenty-first century, demonstrates how the subject has been violated, cut, and objectified.

This is the very altering of identity that fusion involves. This is the connectedness of the subject and the loss of it in a medium. This altering of the subject is part of the connecting process people simply cannot avoid. It happens when the audience is enamored of the jumbotron at sporting events or the television in restaurants. Fusion simulates some reality, which is understood as information, and a person could have the memory of experiencing that world; they would have been in a virtual world, and they are in that world. This is the nature of fusion, which is processual and about subjectivity (real experience) being combined in a process with the virtual, which in turn becomes our experience. Fusion is the flow or flux of being, interwoven and captured by media. People's very nature, which drives them to connect, sets them up for this process and leads them into a world where surely the virtual is real.

# 4

# One or Many Voices

*I LIVE IN A world with many faces and languages, of multiple philoso-*
*phies and modes of being; looking all around helps me to understand*
*there are so many different people. We are all different and unique, as*
*numerous as the many leaves on the trees. There are many voices, so*
*many that sometimes I do not know which one tells the truth. I defi-*
*nitely live in a posttruth world, where everything is relative. I learned*
*in school there are no absolutes. My way of saying that is, "The world*
*is full of contingencies"; according to my teacher in college, that is the*
*case. There is no conspiracy or Big Brother, Google does not know*
*everything I say, and there is no centralized source of knowledge.*
*There is no One World Order, nor one world voice. There are so many*
*varieties of experience it would be impossible for one voice to speak*
*for us all. We do not live in that kind of a world; we do not live in a*
*fictional world. These thoughts were privately spoken in a speculative*
*and stoic way. They were spoken by a doctoral student who did not*
*believe everything said; this person did not think these words were*
*spoken in an idealistic way.*

In the world of media process, the notion of having many
things to choose from, or many voices at play, is an illusion. Media
do not offer many choices but demand that the subject be adherent
to the illusion of choice; it is like experiencing the many colors of a
rainbow but there is only one rainbow. In the face of this univocal,

experiencing reality as being one within the process of fusion, there seems to be choice, but there is no choice. If one has multiple voices calling for attention in this world of flash and frenzy, then it can easily be understood there is a variety of things to choose from and each presents itself serially. In this way these multiple voices could be considered to offer a multivalent world. There are choices offered, but in the life of fusion the variety is funneled into a unified voice.

Univocal means "unambiguous," or "having only one possible meaning." Fusion absorbs the dichotomous and complex into one inseparable texture. For an understanding of what the univocal is, consider the phrase "media are not," as opposed to "media are." In other words media are unmanifest, or exist prior to any experience the subject or person might have; media explicitly undergird the thinking subject. One thinks there is so much variety it must encapsulate the whole. But that is impossible. Therefore some notions and images are not in the scope of choice in media, and therefore reality is not accurately represented. A Lacanian understanding informs the person the whole truth cannot be fully said, known, or represented. There are so many choices offered in the virtual, which leads to the delimitation of choice.

In the fusion process, beings are only certain modes of oneness. The original nature of our way of thinking discriminates between the one and the many; even when one is the desired one, two arise. It seems impossible to escape this dualism; however, dualism is absorbed in fusion. Even the nominal pair virtual/actual collapses or conflates into univocal being. Life is neither dualistic nor pluralistic with all the representations in place within media. Nevertheless, in fusion, life is limited and determined. All live in a univocal world; though there are multiple messages, an overload of choices, a representation of all the choices possible is never complete. Therefore, the choice is limited to what appears on the screen and nothing else; hence, there is only one voice and no choice.

With the univocal, multiple voices not only become one, but they violate the subject because the subject is forced to participate within the univocal. The world can only be what media present to the person in the fusion process. One only agrees with the content of media and nothing outside of their representation. Media lay the whole foundation of our world. Media are prior to any experience. There is no escape from the influence of, and characterizations that are made in, the virtual world. There are no other dimensions and no room for questioning when one is experiencing fusion. It is impossible for one to seek any truth outside of this set. One cannot think beyond the representations that are put in front of them in the fusion process; one becomes that process and does not think for themselves. Presuppositions of media are flat and offer no reality, only virtuality; no world exists except for the land of two-dimensional, flat people. Persons who exist in the virtual are on the flat screen; they represent the becoming of those who participate in media. How can there be difference when no other is involved? In fusion the other is absorbed into a process with the subject, resulting in an absolutely flattened outcome.

Media carry all notions of power because media are omnipotent in the sense that being in media process allows no one access to being outside of media. This demonstrates that media are supraexistent; beyond the simplest or complex understandings of existence, media exist prior to thinking in any category. Media meaning-making is both immanent with and transcendent of our world, preexistent and posterior to the experience of the person. Hence, fusion envelops and violates with its power and supposition. Media exist preeminently and before all other interaction; media dominate the wills of people. Argument is not allowed in fusion, where agreement is the aim.

Because of the many stimuli and the overload of information impressed upon the subject by the media process, it is only possible to see the media version of reality and one's illusion of efficacy. Violation happens when one is presented with an overwhelming amount of information, and the explosion of choice overwhelms the subject; therefore, subjectivity is challenged. Grasping to obtain the illusion is an apparent freedom, but is ultimately the root of suffering. Everything that is present in the fusion process is cause for distress, because of the illusive and unattainable nature of the desired object(s). Jean Baudrillard states: "illusion is the general rule of the universe . . . reality is but an exception . . . absolute truth is the other name for death."[1] The fruits of living in the virtual are inherent in the life of any person because media undergird the conscious and unconscious worlds of existence. That existence is not existence at all, remembering the phrase "media are not." This is the reality of the limitations in the experience of a media-filled world. The virtual is the only thing left to be viable; illusion is what the masses rely on.

One's subjectivity is challenged in the fusion process by the very explicit determination of choice and the unambiguous nature of what is communicated. There is not just a constraint of choice, but an explosion of choice, which overwhelms the subject. The result is the subject has no choice but to accept the summarized version of reality created by the media process. The lack of opinions outside of media are impressed upon the subject by the univocal. The result is a negation of choice and a deflated sense of efficacy. The distortion and dysfunction of screen living, the lack of efficacy, leads one to the conclusion the content of that person's real world is infinitely limited. This leads to a great deception, that the only world without limits is the virtual world; therefore it is conceived of as the better world. The virtual has become the real world preeminently.

When considering the state of experience and the senses involved with media engagement, it becomes apparent the whole body is not involved. The subject uses sight and/or hearing to experience media of many types. In fusion the perceived choice deadens thinking, and its flashes and bytes deaden the senses. This is dangerous and problematic because it engenders media with the power to determine, objectify, and do violence to bodies. One becomes what they participate in, unwillingly; there really is no choice. The world of media lends to unhealthy expectations about the body that have been noted for decades.

The subject is not *a priori* the basis of reality but the manifestation of media. There can be no experience outside of media; one is embedded in it early in life. There is no escape from media's representations. The pervasiveness of media destabilizes the sense of subjectivity. Hence, violence is committed against the subject when only oneness is found in a multitude of seeming choices.

---

1. Baudrillard, *Vital Illusion*, 72.

The subject is the prey of media; fusion totalizes the multivalent or summarizes all possible outcomes into one result, which then becomes the virtual reality. This virtual singular reality is more real than reality.

An issue fusion brings out involves the nature of will and desire. So the question arises: How much power does the person have in determining their world? The resulting consideration about the process of experience and media prompts one to consider how the subject works. Stanislaw M. Ulam wrote about the multiplicity that makes up the self, not just the dualisms of body/mind or subject/object. Ulam states: "It is really a multi-person game, but consciously the appearance is of a one-dimensional, purely temporal sequence. One is only consciously aware of the something in the brain which acts as a summarizer or totalizer of the process going on and that probably consists of many parts acting simultaneously on each other."[2] This statement about consciousness is insightful and also contributes to our understanding what happens in media process.

That intersubjective moment, of media swallowing up the subject, brings the cacophony of voices and choices into a unified form. The subject, being originally selfish, attempts to please itself and abate its desire by seeking something (perhaps a oneness) which will fulfill its desire, being that the one it loves is the other. The other is a reflection of the subject itself and leads the subject to an ouroboros-like path back to itself. This circular nature of desire sends the subject into itself in isolation, disconnecting the person from the real and physical world. The relationship between knowledge and power is strikingly more connected to the process of meeting desire. Actually, knowledge and choice lead to less power, because the only choice that exists is media's oneness, which is no choice at all.

The nature of the relationship with media is the lack of self-determination disguised as freedom. Media are the one which involve the particular and the many. The power of the individual is equivalent to the language which structures the unconscious. Lacan demonstratively states: "The unconscious is structured like

---

2. Ulam, *Adventures of a Mathematician*, 180.

a language."[3] The language of the unconscious is media representation. We live in a time where our memories and aspirations have been inculcated with media. A person cannot even think without reference to media. This is termed "digitized thought" and demonstrates the power of media to confiscate the power of the psyche. The person and their other (which is a misnomer) contain, through media, an unfathomable language of representations, to the degree these representations are seen and heard everywhere.

Relationship has a wide range of emotion and cognition, and all of it is formulated in media. In the case of the subjective experience in media process, it must be understood that the narrative is all about you. In the commercial and political realms, the message is that it is all about you! There is no privation but rather promise of gain. Ironically, the isolation one feels is privation through selfishness. With all the stimuli presented by media, it is impossible for the subject not to focus, inwardly and with fascination, on the multiple. However, singularity is none other than multiple, in the deepest part of the person.

It is not the multiple subjects but rather each individual that gets entrapped through fusion. The individual becomes one part of a whole into which subjective experience is lost. Then the effect on the individual is of no consequence; personhood no longer exists. The seductive nature, as Baudrillard would have it, offers choices not just hosting a whole population; media are picking persons out as individuals and certain communities to react to their persuasiveness. Again the subject is violated by media, and fusion brings about a deflated sense of self-efficacy. Even though there are a multitude of people and differences, there is a oneness of the reality which is created. This ensures the effect of media; even though media offer supposed diversity, media speak from one position. That one position traps the subject, and through the process engages the subject with the illusion of multiplicity. The one position objectifies all experience into media process.

When the person watches the screen, they are living the life that only has the representations which are offered by media;

8. Lacan, *Four Fundamental Concepts*, 203.

nothing is allowed beyond what is presented. By the fusion process the person is seduced to make the choice that is possible, which is no choice at all. As the screen presents the virtual, a conflation of the virtual and the actual takes place, which means the delimiting of choice. In actuality there is no choice; in the virtual world there is a multitude of representations from which to choose but there is no choosing power, no efficacy. There is no actuality, because the virtual exists first and is that which separates the subject from its relationship with its other.

Slavoj Žižek states: "The abyss of the depth of another personality, its utter impenetrability—first found its full expression in Judaism, with its injunction to love your neighbor as yourself."[4] Though persons may be our physical neighbors, close in actual proximity, being engrossed in media means they are not neighbors at all. Levinas thought of this neighbor as an abysmal point of reference. There is no neighbor to love, no self to love, only the projection of virtuality. How can there be difference when no *other* is involved? Fusion creates and maintains an existentially lonely place. The app one is interested in fulfills the tendentious nature of loneliness, albeit temporarily.

---

4. Žižek, *How to Read Lacan*, 25.

# 5

# The Violence of Virtuality

*THE SMELL AND THE surrounding sounds that create what she experiences; these have an effect on her emotions and embrace her like a warming and comforting blanket. The element of surprise and the anticipation and suspense that enthrall her heart determine its palpitations. She is plugged in, the connection completely seamless, the waves of sound and decibels fill her body with vibrations. Her perspective is the only one in the room, though she detects the movements of the others in her presence.*

*The smallest sound from outside of her experience she considers to be a frustrating interruption of her blissful escape; a sentimental moment which tugs at her causes a tingling sensation in her scalp. With her body slightly tense, she enters a scene with her favorite character, expecting a suspenseful moment, and abruptly music and color confirm her emotions. Enveloped in a dark moment, the squealing of a wheel and a screaming voice wrench at her nervous system as she exits the scene as quickly as she had entered it. The senses that had utilized her are far more than sight and sound. She feels like exiting while she presses herself into her seat.*

*Her heart throbs upon entering the hall of the big screen, and she experiences a warm glow in her own personal space. Quick, riveting scenes engage and require attention, though little of it. A violent scene violates and slaps the face; a love scene caresses the heart. Production has moved its representations into the field of the psyche. There is style, status, expression, desire. This desire folds into her subjective experience and media also engage her, as her consciousness swims in the information, data, and pixels, with no escape and no desire for escape.* The process between the person and media has been referred to as fusion and takes place in the subjective domain. The subject is something that exists as a psychological and philosophical phenomenon or entity, which is susceptible to being taken over by an object, that is, an object which is external to the subject. That object in this case is media, which has the power to overwhelm the subject. Media's takeover of the subject is not liberating, but rather is a violation. Media are not negative or positive in the colloquial sense, as in unhealthy or healthy. Media are positive only in the sense that they are positively invasive and violating. Media have the characteristics of a monopoly in the marketplace or an intruder waiting to raid the soul of a person. Media are the object referred to above; media are encroaching on the mental territory of the population of the world.

Media engage the person in this creative process. A person can create their identity from media, but not from within; the moment one is exposed to media, the person has already been seduced or violated. One is at first and then always exposed to media; this is an inescapable fact once at a very early age the person is subjected to invasive media. Lacan, however, explained identity is formed when a child looks in a mirror and realizes they are the intrinsic thing controlling an otherwise chance collection of body parts, limbs, appendages, and the like. As Adrian Johnston explains, "the ego, despite conscious senses to the contrary, is not a locus of autonomous agency, the seat of a free, true 'I' determining its own fate."[1] This "true 'I'" is the ego which is a phenomenon, a step removed from the subject, and is a mere illusion.

Until there was the mirror experience, there was no sense of a unified entity which controls the person. At the breach of that experience, it is in that sense of control which the ego is formed. This is a process that runs parallel to the notion of fusion, where a person's constructed sense of control is formed by media or indeed is media.

1. Johnston, "Jacques Lacan," sec. 2.2, line 7.

The sense of control, the ego, or the person's identity is a result of a process, be it the mirror stage or the fusion process. Persons do not create themselves *ex nihilo*, out of nothing, but the material they use is already constructed by society, family, or media. A simple turn to the subject as deconstructed is only the first step in the creative process. Constructivism can be used as a tool in creativity, but it is likely the person who is constructing is basing their ideas on ideations they were exposed to. Often the ideations come from someone in power, like a celebrity or a politician. The problem lies in the person thinking they are creating and constructing in a vacuum and their ideas came from within them, when in fact they likely came from an outside source.

The work a poet or screenwriter produces, or the end result seen in video games and music videos, is often quite spectacular; the colors, the verbiage, light and shading, the textures and connotations—all seduce and entrap the experience or the subject of the audience. This process becomes the audience, or the audience becomes the process. It is a question of what will win the attention. The service that is provided to the viewer and the experience afforded the consumer are objects of a higher order; these are generally considered to be matchless, timely, and timeless. To put it another way, fusion is a process involving elimination of the primacy of the subject, the overpowering of subject. An audience at a media event is full of literally captive persons. There is no room for any other process and content outside of the interrelationship of subject and media. The subject is vaporized into the process and it reaches its horizon in the object: media.

In the fusion process individuals are not self-examiners of their own functioning. The individual does not pose a threat to the process, but fusion does more than simply something similar to threatening the person; it enthralls through the weakness of the subject. Weakness is not just evidenced through some effort to overpower. Fusion happens through enticement, persuasion, and violation. Coercion and seduction are terms that accurately describe the effect of media on the singular person. The fusion process is a much more subtle and entangling process which is not easily reduced to a fixed power relationship. Fusion is not simply a result of hegemonic forces or a hierarchically structured society. This process is in fact a subjugating subjective force both within and outside the individual, and has content that is not in the subject's control. Therefore, it is a violation of one's very own dignity.

Fusion is similar to the process that Kaja Silverman describes as *suture* in her work, *The Subject of Semiotics*.[2] This term, suture, involves the juxtaposition of an onlooker to a movie, but has the connotation of a surgeon stitching together a wound. The notion is derived from the affiliation of the subject to its object of desire in a Lacanian sense. It can be considered, in the work of Gilles Deleuze or Jean Baudrillard, a sense of desiring connection with the desiring-machine (in Deleuze) or the screen (in Baudrillard) which causes one to be in relationship to another and in relationship to the material world or world of ideas. One looks to media connection to obtain relationship. As long as our lives feature modern media, there will be the tendency to look there for self and other, through media. Desiring the other or oneself is the first step toward self-creation, but in this day and age it does not start outside of media construction.

The difficulty in using Baudrillard and Deleuze side by side is there is a sticking point described by Baudrillard himself in the short phrase: "everything started with seduction, not with desire."[3] For Deleuze everything starts with the desire; the subject is a remnant of desiring production. For Baudrillard the subject is fragile and is seduced by media. Once seduced there is no separation, no alterity. For Baudrillard there is representation of desire in the object, yet it is really seduction at work. Deleuze sees it a bit differently; everything is desire. Deleuze pronounces the definition of the person to happen by and in conjunction with desire, whereas Baudrillard glances at desire but readily moves to seduction. Baudrillard states: "Only that which no longer poses the problem of its own desire . . . is seductive, only that which has passed through the absolution and resolution of its own desire."[4]

---

2. Silverman, *Subject of Semiotics*, 247.
3. Baudrillard, *Fatal Strategies*, 111.
4. Baudrillard, *Fatal Strategies*, 120.

Deleuze's analysis is that being is sensual, while Baudrillard remains with the representation of the sensual. Deleuze writes about the "being of sensation,"[5] not like data being discursively packaged and giving unity to the manifold, but rather being involves sensation with no union of all the senses. Desire is, with or without representation. The position of Baudrillard would be that representation precedes desire and in fact creates it. All of this discussion rests on the underlying presupposition of a dichotomy between subject and object, desire and representation.

Perhaps it may seem these two philosophical positions cannot be rectified but desire and seduction can and do indeed work together. Baudrillard peers within the nature of relationship and finds reality at play, theatrical and representational. This comes during an effort to reconcile the subject and the object. Baudrillard finds our knowledge of this nature of reality in a decline, a death proportionate to entropy, a "death of reality."[6]

For Deleuze the expression of desire is a process that is alive with connections. With certainty, seriousness, and solemnity, Baudrillard propounds that the world is "the radical impossibility of a real presence of things or beings, their definitive absence from themselves."[7] Baudrillard extends that notion by writing "we are never exactly present to ourselves, or to others. Thus we are not exactly real for one another, nor are we quite real to ourselves. And this radical alterity is our best chance—our best chance of attracting and being attracted to others, of seducing and being seduced. Put simply our chance at life."[8] Baudrillard also stresses this matter of the seduction the individual is exposed to when viewing or participating in media. He states it in the following fashion:

> In our philosophy of desire, the subject retains an absolute privilege, since it is the subject that desires. But everything is inverted if one passes on to the thought of seduction. There, it's no longer the subject which desires,

5. Deleuze and Guattari, *What is Philosophy?*, 178.

6. Baudrillard, *Simulacra and Simulation*, 28.

7. Baudrillard, *Vital Illusion*, 70–71.

8. Baudrillard, *Vital Illusion*, 71.

it's the object which seduces. Everything comes from the object and everything returns to it, just as everything started with seduction, not with desire.[9]

According to Baudrillard, the meaning-making apparatus is seductive. Baudrillard asks, "Is it not rather the seducer who is seduced, and does the initiative not revert secretly to the object? The seducer believes he envelops it in his strategy, but he is caught by the lure of this banal strategy and it is rather the object that envelops him in its fatal strategy."[10] In order for the object to be desired the seducer seduces itself.

Henceforth, the ultimate object, manipulated by a subject, becomes the lover of the subject. This exercise is construed as banal, and Baudrillard states "everything started with seduction."[11] This is how fusion begins; and the further the seduction and introjections, the further the process multiplies. Fusion is not just a stitching together, or a connection, but a drowning of the self or soul in a pixilated virtual and demeaning process, which is fusion. By watching the screens everywhere one goes, they become enmeshed with media process, and the subject is taken over. In fusion there is no new subject or object but only the activated field of nondistinction. If the object is the seducer, who is behind the curtain? Who manipulates the pixels? Media are the objectifiers par excellence which seduce the other through the manipulation of the other as an object. Deception and seduction administer this virtual love. Is desire self-fulfilling, or are the masses further and further seduced by the pixilated age into deception? Is this where our desire is leading us?

There is the body of media which enables the seductive field of play. In this field there is action, play, violence, and seduction all in virtuality. Qualitative worlds when quantified and digitized have their horizons stretched by language and graphics at the expense of tangibility. Caressing becomes virtual beauty beyond the reach of the lover. The beloved is an object of desire adjusted by pixel values, quantitatively. The globalizing phenomenon has digitized

9. Baudrillard, *Fatal Strategies*, 111.

10. Baudrillard, *Fatal Strategies*, 120.

11. Baudrillard, *Fatal Strategies*, 111.

and pixilated our reality and stops at nothing, feeding us violence and subjugation every day. This is a world of desire for violence, and a world of individuated selves existing within the envelopment of the virtual. At a very innocent time in their lives, children are being exposed to graphic violence and ingrained with the notion that morality is relative and mores are meaningless. It is the intentionality and subversiveness of media that makes use of fusion and is an active force at work. Indeed the taking over of each subject by media (not necessarily objective) is violence. They just sit by and gaze.

In fusion the subject becomes process, once and for all transgressed, subjugated, and eliminated. Baudrillard states:

> knowledge defined conventionally, always proceeds in the same direction, from the subject to the object. But today processes of reversion are emerging everywhere . . . This duel engaged in by the subject and the object means the loss of the subject's hegemonic position: the object becomes the horizon of the subject's disappearance.[12]

It should be noted that from the very beginning of a life, beginning in 1995, a person has no other baggage to bring to a medium than that very meaning-making apparatus of larger media or a particular medium itself. This is not some cry like "Rock-n-Roll is evil;" this is a matter of our survival as real people, our credibility as humans on the green earth. The human is dying and the machines of meaning-making, though partly created and definitely perpetuated by us, are killing us off. The world's people are being trapped by each medium as individuals relish in it.

Lifeblood is only necessary to keep the organism alive, and admittedly the human brain, but that very brain is being captured by every pixel it integrates. The idea of artificial intelligence, or even practical intelligence, is being tampered with and trampled by the largest machine ever, and there seems to be no way to stop its process. Fusion is salient to our expectations of our inner life and corporeal experience, not to mention our body image, and all are representations of media. Not only are people defined by fusion; they are violated by it. The masses are melded to the massive

12. Baudrillard, *Vital Illusion*, 76.

media machine, with its array of flickers and flashes. Their bodies disappear and are replaced, or expectations about their bodies are changed forever. There is only one body—the body of media—lavishing over it and weeping at the sight of one's own body. There is no point of reference, no two sides to compare or contrast. There is no dialectic, for any dialectic, along with the dialectic of history, is destroyed by virtuality.

# 6

# Thinking and the Screen

*HEY! I WAS WATCHING this documentary/film of how ridiculous religion and religious life is, and the presenter was a well-known television figure. Wow! He interviewed people around the world, and that increases the credibility of his work. The presenter was excellent in the way he communicated and asked people questions. This guy really knows all about religion and is really down on religious studies. He knows so much and passes his knowledge along to others. Frankly, I am tired of having religion pushed on me by self-righteous people. I know now that religion is irrational and has beliefs held by irrational people. After watching this show I know so much about religion that I can beat down any Bible-thumping idiot I meet. I used my search engine a lot to get to the sources he used and they all were on internet encyclopedias. He was so right about everything. Every time I used my search engine to find something the coolest thing happened. I was drawn by my internet experience to so many other resources; my search engine is so intuitive and vast with connections to so much knowledge. I now know everything. All knowledge is at my fingertips. Anytime some religious person talks to me I can just tear them up with my vast knowledge.*

Media ushered in a way of thinking in flash and multiple frames of experience. Thinking, as an experience of television and internet, has continuously exposed the person to the same content with the same messages. To be full of knowledge is to be fused to the screen. Peter Sacks asks, then explains: "Is it true that higher education does not work anymore? It doesn't challenge . . . Machines are easier. If we can get it from machines we do not have to get it from a person . . . the media are passive . . . safer. It doesn't really affect us. But a teacher, it's real, it's close."[1] The postmodern has had an effect on the next generations that have arisen with grossly different perceptual needs and with machines (screens and computers) to feed their desires.

Devices perpetuate the constant flow of reality, making virtual reality realer than real and a machinistic and screen-oriented reality. The wonder of truth comes fully from the screen that places all problems of consistency, computability, and decidability in the hands of media. In fact, as Lawson states, Jacques Derrida's "abandonment of decidability would at first sight imply the end of the search for knowledge and truth."[2] With media in place there is no need for searching; truth is only for the compliant, and it is all the same. David Hume was empirically suggestive of the idea that the person perceives a world of phenomena that can only be simply known as immediate and not beyond one's own knowing, indeed the sensuous world, impressions are reality. Knowledge obtained through substantiated touch, taste, or auditory systems, although discovered empirically by the bodies' sensual experiences, is considered suspect. In the latest way of understanding life, knowledge must reach persons through media experience before it can be considered valid knowledge.

In the twenty-first century, people find many truths in media, such as medical, psychological, and philosophical truths. In a post-truth world where everything is relative, the promise of truth is appealing and necessary. One violated by fusion believes the truths presented in media and lives in those truths, which are considered absolutes. The question of how to find truths in a world of relativism is solved by media. These truths come to one as research-based or through the experience of the other; they are valid and beyond reprehension because they have become part of one's subjectivity.

1. Sacks, *Generation X*, 145.
2. Lawson, *Reflexivity*, 121.

The subject is literally a captive audience. Once one is fused into the process there is no escape. The power of fusion calls up Orwellian truth, in the mind of the cultural critic. As Lacan demonstrated, one cannot know the real. In these times, through fusion it is apparent the virtual is known, but nothing that is real can be known. In much the same way that the subject goes under subversion by fusion, so do the person's senses. Media play a game with our senses when the fusion process takes place; our subjective and sensory experience is abducted by fusion. So when one doubts the real in favor of the virtual, the realer than real, isn't one then not doing what René Descartes did, in essence? Doubting, more doubting, and denial happen, until consciousness has a body shape like that of the box, flat and thin like a screen.

This denial of the tangible world and way of thinking is contrary to print and verbiage as the means to structure consciousness. Culture has spread through virtual means, which has become the primary understanding of ritual. The one who challenges classical truths does so through the power of media. In the twenty-first century, the transmission of cultural knowledge is passed on through the screen, not through metaphor, but through image. This knowledge is the image of the imagination influenced by graphic representation. Culture has abandoned text in favor of sound bytes and images. Persons no longer think, but wait for images to be put in front of them or embedded in their subjective process. Media force us into a process that one might consider thinking, when in fact it is this process, fusion (the melding together of the subject and media) that gives so-called absolute truth and is totalizing in nature. The dialectic disappears when the process begins, for there is no outside force. Fusion is all there is to be experienced; this fusion is our everyday experience. It is practically impossible to escape.

Baudrillard introduces us to the notion of knowledge being destroyed and deconstructed by media. Baudrillard explains:

> In the domain of the illusion, knowledge is no longer logically possible, for its principles and postulates cannot function. And this is not just a metaphysical insight: today the microsciences stand at the point where the object as such no longer exists. It vanishes, it escapes, it has no

definite status, it only appears in the form of ephemeral and aleatory traces on the screens of virtualization.[3]

We have succeeded in pushing aside the imagination in favor of manipulation. Fusion is a trap that closes in on us with its titillation and perfect images from which the subject has no escape. In trapping the subject in the domain of illusion, media have done to persons what has been done throughout history to animals. Actions are symbolic of the condition in which persons find themselves, trapped by the illusion that these acts are derived from freedom. Persons have affective life rather like the behavior of animals in the fight-or-flight mode of existence. Indeed, rather than engaging in the presumed free thought afforded the individual by media, which is not freedom at all, persons are engaging in actions that are more akin to those of caged animals. The price for so-called free thought is the dearth of media, illusion. Just as one sees themselves making gains in freedom, it is in fact media reigning in thought and imagination by use of the machine: the screen. Deleuze states: "nothing is done by the imagination; everything is done in the imagination. It is not even a faculty for forming ideas, because the production of an idea by the imagination is only the reproduction of an impression in the imagination."[4] Thought, whether conscious or unconscious, is structured, from the birth of the screen, by image of the immaterial. This ghostlike imagery fails to substantiate intelligibility, but sends the individual down the path of stagnation and offense. Violence is the very trapping of the subject by media: fusion.

This violence brings out the nature of media's use of knowledge to confound ritual. There has been a shift in the way persons are conscious of knowledge. The experience of media as thought has been through perfection, distortion, and binding of the imagination. The perfection and pixilation has distorted reasoning to the extent that there is no reason, but rather the infiltration of media images into culture. This is the way ritual knowledge has been usurped by media and turned toward phenomena like commercialization. Culture no longer has propaganda but rather the instilling

3. Baudrillard, *Vital Illusion*, 75.
4. Deleuze, *Empiricism and Subjectivity*, 23.

of various modes of representation, such as commercials, which the masses are exposed to. The subject loses power, meaning that, as Theodor W. Adorno states: "advertising becomes information when there is no longer anything to choose from, when the recognition of brand names has taken the place of choice."[5] Fusion has endorsed the status quo of advertising, so each new image is treated as arcane.

The Marxist dialectic preserves history; this happens as well in the Hegelian model, always allowing for an antithesis to the thesis and the continuation of the process, whereby there is a movement to synthesis. The issue at stake here is whether or not world history can be defined by dialectic outside of the solipsistic view of media, which is the body of media and media representation of history. The end of history began with the turn to the subject; as it stands now, media bring the end of history. The media-defined world is determined by media perspective, whereby the individual life is well defined by fusion. It is noted the history of the world is defined by media. With fusion, the individual experiences media's version of history as a part of their subjectivity. This is the nature of fusion and suggests our world and history are subjective. Moreover, subjectivity is determined by media and any attempts to make it otherwise are unredeemed. The world is constructed as media make it out to be. The individual can yearn to have power of its own to determine what reality will be; often, though, the individual cannot make a distinction between some wish about reality and the determined nature of how things come into being by force of media.

How does history's dialectic get lost in media? How is it the dialectic which Georg Wilhelm Friedrich Hegel and Karl Marx identify as the process through which history passes becomes enveloped by the singularly focused drive or seduction of this media machine? Foucault suggested history has breaks, suggesting it is not linear. According to Foucault, each episteme, or stage of history, is not necessarily connected linearly to the previous one. No matter how linear or broken the sequences of history may be, it all resolves itself in the univocity of media. History loses its power when media make everything relative. The so-called leveling of the playing field

5. Adorno, *Culture Industry*, 85.

makes everything become irrelevant. This happens as a result of globalization. History is no more when the dictates of media construct its significances. History is denied the opportunity to blossom from dialectic when the one within history no longer knows of or contributes to its destiny. History has no intention because media are diffuse and disparate. Dispirited, there is no zeitgeist, but a flood of ideas, notions, and disjoined verbiage and imagery. How then has it come to this end of history? The answer is through relinquishing the power to define, media have taken over and things have since been under media's control.

The end of history is the tool of the hostile and violating subject-media process. The body human, the body as subject and object, and the body of media all get an examination for their effectuality upon each other. This is done through media meaning-making; the advancement of fusion is upon individuals and their relationships. This is exactly where the screen weaver, that one with which there is no folly, meets up with the postmodern paradigm. The postmodern movement toward no truth gives inroads for the manipulation of bodies, virtual bodies, by media, which prescribe to all and inscribe on their territories their notions. Ritual has been replaced by media; there are new myths to support media events with their global effects and illustrious information sharing instead of truth sharing. Baudrillard exclaims, "You don't have to be politically aware to realize that, after the famous dustbins of history, we are now seeing the dustbins of information. Now, information may well be a myth, but this alternative myth, the modern substitute for all other values, has been rammed down our throats incessantly."[6] Persons then understand truth comes from their singular, isolated, and violated self, which is the experience of media. As philosophers like Richard Rorty[7] and Hilary Lawson[8] have noted, objectivity and empiricism no longer preside over the postmodern world and its condition, but rather contingency and relativity. Therefore, the body in the real world feels foreign and one feels dissociated; that is the result of fusion.

6. Baudrillard, *Screened Out*, 189.

7. Rorty, *Irony, Contingency, and Solidarity*.

8. Lawson, *Reflexivity*.

# 7

# Real Fun

*My avatar is for fighting with weapons in this first-person perspective, first-person shooter game. This is real combat! War against the zombie uprising and upstart. As she floats upward, weirdly leaving a trail of smoke and dirt or a whirlwind and dust cloud below, she is rising to the ceiling of the pavilion in the compound, while soldiers of the other await her curse, command, or blessing. My call and duty is to defeat and dismember as many zombies as possible. I crouch outside in my post with my Magnum in its holster, whereby I may reach it just over my left shoulder and my automatic weapon held firmly against my right thigh. I am ready to kill . . . this is no game. If the other's soldiers are going to take us on, they will win over my dead body. I intend to ace an objective kill. There are 10 million players in this game, this war, and I intend to see a lot of heads tumble and pink splatter on my goggles. If she had not started this zombie craze it would not be worth so many lives to be stolen. If I can only be as dedicated as the most dedicated of soldier and sacrifice myself, I will; I see six barrels which I can access in order to kill other soldiers. As I plow through this labyrinth of a hole and find the commander to rescue, I avoid the demon lord. I have as my assets: fighting, accuracy, and weapons.*

The vignette above features a constructed world where a person is engrossed in the game to the extent that it becomes real. One might ask: Is there a reality which is not constructed? It might not be clear which worlds are constructed and which are not, but it is clear games are constructed realities: hence the term "gaming." In this postmodern world, or posttruth world, one knows not whether something is a lie or a fact. To the constructivist and to the deconstructionist there is no central truth lending to the notion of a reality that is not constructed. Many take comfort in the notion that there is no absoluteness; therefore, any position is to be regarded with the same consideration as being true as any other. However, this is a challenging position because in the postmodern world many now are seeking "truth" eagerly out of a need and yearning for security. Truth and reality are preciously sought out in the fallout of postmodern relativism. There was the desire for everyone's truths to matter, but now there is the pursuit of truth because people fear the implications of relativism. It implies that if everything is relative then nothing exists in and of itself. That means there is emptiness and insecurity to deal with. Boredom and emptiness are averted through the use of games and other media; desire for meaning drives this necessity. In the common household, emptiness and lack of stimulation is intolerable; therefore, the television and computers continue to play while someone is at home (and sometimes when no one but the pets is at home). Media are necessary for life; no one lives unless they are plugged into a device.

One can go to the screen and play a violent video game with some stranger on the other side of the world. Once one is into a game, there is no escape from the veracity of the realness and the feel of the fit a person has for their surroundings, the environment, or the host. Gaming is reality for the person experiencing the temptation to go into attack mode and take out the enemy. It is through this experience that pseudo-efficacy, which fosters the sense of ultimate control, guarantees power and security. The participant need only react with the flesh and bones of their fingers in order to experience, view, and hear the world of the screen. This is more than a philosophical position; it is a reality. Many individuals remain fused to their particular "chosen" world and cannot escape thoughts of it throughout their day.

Being fused to a screen, movie, or game can happen without helpful time management; neither young people nor children have a chance of learning anything other than the content of their game, and the game can be potentially reprehensible. Children of all ages play violent video games, and many adults do also; the internet is a place to meet and make friends who remain anonymous or pseudonymous, which can become a snare or trap for seemingly innocent or naïve persons who may meet seemingly dangerous persons with harmful intent. Limited education is afforded outside of the screen opportunities one is involved in; even so, video games have become quite the sport and even find their way into venues next to physical sports.

Studying media can demonstrate multiple instances of how media influence society to participate in such virtual meaning-making activities as games. One model for understanding media, meaning-making, and behavior, called the Social Meaning Framework, has been developed by Shane Murphy, who states: "The perceived meaning of game play will determine subsequent changes in self-efficacy, perceived ability and enjoyment and it is these psychological factors that the Social Meaning Framework predicts will influence subsequent behavior."[1] This theoretical positioning explains that through the process of playing games on a computer or gaming system, persons can gain skills and pleasurable time; it also suggests some connection between media, meaning, and personal subjective experience. Games have the potential to invade and seduce the subject because of their interactive nature. This interactivity fosters the perception of mastery and control, even though this mastery is imaginary; this is the dynamic which sets the person up for entrapment by media. The more static or less interactive and dynamic the medium is, the less it operates in a process manner. The idea is when one comes to a media device there is more than a glance or even a stare, but an entrapment much stronger than a simple connection. When the subject of a person connects with an object, it loses its subjective nature and becomes objectified. When the subject of a person connects with media, it loses any nature it may have of its

---

1. Murphy, "Social Meaning Framework," 1.

own and becomes process. This process is the interaction between subject and media. It is at once subject and media; the person is trapped in the process. The subverted subject acts on behalf of and is controlled by the particular medium.

It is media's process that is most powerful, rather than the content it presents. However content, whether enhancing or dangerous, might be very powerful as well. Nine out of ten teen adult video games include violent activities and scenarios. The main concern with fusion is it involves the seduction of the person or subject into the media event in a complete way. The subject loses its identity in media during the fusion process. This can lead to a dissociative state whereby the subject understands themselves to have more than one persona. The actual state of fusion involves the dissolution or dissolving of the subject into the event to the extent that the identity of the original subject no longer exists; instead, the subject becomes the character within the game or virtual reality. The reality of the virtual becomes the reality of the person. The person is absorbed into the virtual and becomes the other.

In the case of violence within video gaming, the person becomes the violent character. Once a connection is established, an effect lingers. The media process remains with the individual, because the nature of media is that it precedes one's existence. The person is in media, as a fish in water. The masses are in such a state as to be unaware of the reality that they are swimming in media and do not make a distinction between themselves and media. The subject becomes the other in the Lacanian sense. Identity is eclipsed and masses meet their identity through the subject-media process.

The subject playing an identity within the game takes on the beliefs of the game's reality. The person carries with them, outside of the game, the reality of the gaming experience to the extent that the distinction between subject and object, real or virtual, is not clear at all. Fusion causes the person to be lost in their new identity and the created world around it. Media have invaded the very life of the individual and the person has become the subject of media. The blurred lines can offer rewards like developing the ability to harm or kill others in any reality. When given a lot of time, adeptness is part of learning to kill in the gaming world. The problem is since each person is already swimming in media, which carry the master narrative for the person, they will be unable to avoid being entraps them daily. Harming others and believing one has many lives supports some kind of belief in a constructed immortality. Lives are built up in accordance with the number of points or the power one accumulates in a particular game scenario.

The relationship between violence and violent video games has been an ongoing discussion for some time. An understanding of the subject-media process and fusion help us procure some answers to these questions. When the subject is eclipsed by an object or media, whereby the subject becomes objectified, the control and efficacy once owned by the subject are compromised, and the result could be that the virtual lived experience will makes its way into the world of flesh and blood. On the other hand, one must consider there is no distinction between virtual and actual; the subject-media process has secured the reality of the masses as actual becomes the virtual and therefore all is virtual. After this realization, that one is trapped in the virtual, the implications of gaming and virtual reality are strongly on the side of understanding the danger of the game world.

Again, Murphy notes that internet games "strive to recreate the complexities of societies at war and online battles can involve hundreds of participants at a time."[2] This striving is not in vain, because these simulations are quite accurate. The technology used for virtual reality and gaming is sophisticated enough to be used for certain military operations. It is the assumed or virtual knowledge that presents as real in media of all kinds. Nonetheless, knowledge is distinctly linked to power, as explained by renowned philosophers like John Locke, Michel Foucault, Aldous Huxley, and many others. There is in the gaming venue a source of illusory skillfulness and purpose. One adept in playing video games accepts a different kind of talent and intelligence. Knowledge of gaming is valued because the production of games is a huge industry. Each person vetted in video games feels as though they are special persons with experience in the creative knowledge that can be used by the industry.

2. Murphy, "Social Meaning Framework," 7.

Sadly, not every gamer is talented enough to create those games that fuel the habits of other gamers. There seems to be the need for creating content that will extend and sustain playing time. Video games are now considered a sport and a lucrative industry; it can be noted that video games are promoted on social media as well. Though jobs are created, minds also become trapped in the wonders and often the violence of game playing.

Game playing on the internet is an example of how one can become lost in media and enclosed in a game—trapped, not as an addiction, but as seduction and a venomous strike by a force that is wildly out of the control of the individual. There is no way possible for the gamer to escape the game upon being seduced; once in the terrain and landscape of the life of the game, that reality is at once generated and manifest in the mind of the gamer. Many never leave the game because they perpetuate it in their minds throughout their real life.

Content of the game is tracked through assumed channels or virtual knowledge that presents as real in media of all kinds. The virtual, to the gamer, is real and perhaps too real. In this environment of virtual reality the gamer takes on an avatar through which that person gains friends and relationships. One's relationships are suspect because the real identities are not verifiable. The virtual can be "realer than real" in the words of Massumi. Through the subject-media process many are caught in gaming reality or realities. Every moment of the day the gamer spends their time either playing or scheming, some so attached to the extent as to have general apathy about real life.

From environmental education to space exploration, virtual reality has been used in the classroom. Virtual reality has been used to aid people in experiencing exotic places. Virtual reality is a form of media which interrogates the perception of the real, leaving aside the experience of the real world. Virtual reality may not mean the imitation of the real. Žižek expresses that "Virtual Reality in itself is a rather miserable idea: that of imitating reality, of reproducing its experience in an artificial medium."[3] Plain old duplication is not

3. Žižek, *Organs Without Bodies*, 3.

what virtual reality implies in the sense of the self and the fragility of the subject. That which is occurring here is the pretentions of the self, or rather the intentions of the self or subjective experience. Žižek gives the example of a rat that is synergistically connected to a device which sends a preceding inclination to the brain and each inclination leads to the expected behavior. The question is whether a person, given one's ability to reflect on one's own behavior, seems to oneself to be controlled by a meaning-making machine. Each individual subject is given intention by media, of which the subject is unaware or conscious.

Fusion is when the individual enters the virtual world process unwittingly and experiences a loss during the process. Game playing on the internet is an example of how one can become lost in media. Murphy explains, "Two, three or four players could play the same game side-by-side, and games of a social nature . . . were designed with this technology in mind, especially during and since the Powerful Home Console Era."[4] There are many examples of game playing in which the individual takes on the role of hero, savior, or villain. Many of the games involve destruction and murder or warfare. A common point here in Murphy's statement is the individual plays "games of a social nature." He goes on to write that the "characteristic of online social games is that they encourage the formation of close and long-term relationships."[5] In fact, these are virtual, not social, relationships. They may exist over long periods of time, but until the individuals meet in person, the relationship, it seems, remains only a virtual one. Because these relations are not social in nature but rather virtual, they can be quite deceptive. The actual person at the other media device can have any identity, while maintaining a virtual identity online. These relations can involve many individuals from anywhere on earth.

4. Murphy, "Social Meaning Framework," 5.
5. Murphy, "Social Meaning Framework," 7.

# 8

# The Real and Relationship

*I PUT INFORMATION ON the dating app in or order to attract women whom I might be interested in. I tweaked a few things, I admit, so that I would find some common ground for discussion with someone. It is not like I do not know a lot about the things I mentioned on the app; it is more likely that I am providind a broad base of interests in such a way that I get a bite from an intelligent woman. I could email her, once she identifies her interests, with the knowledge I have in certain areas even though these interests do not particularly make me happy. I just want to find a woman to date and I am not going to great lengths to find one. Most people on these apps just want to hook up; I could see this going further for me. I want to find a woman, but I am fearful of what or who I might find.*

I have been looking for a man who identifies with social causes and who seems to be the one. After reading about you I have found an interest and have gotten up the nerve to write you. Please tell me the thing you feel most passionate about.

*Should I write this one back or is her reply to my bio too short? I have had a few weird replies that were lengthy and demonstrated some incompetence in the areas I am interested in. This one, though brief, shows an interest in something I know about. However, my political beliefs are conservative, so I should keep on my toes when talking to her.*

Dear Peggy,

    I am writing you to let you know how interesting you are; I would like to meet you. I am looking for a long-term relationship. Are you? Our interests line up. I love to discuss how stupid people are for neglecting things that need to happen to liberate the poor. I hope we can get together and discuss things like this; when I read your bio I wondered where you stood politically. We definitely are a match on that topic. How would you like to get coffee sometime? We could meet at the coffee shop on 3rd and Jackson Streets. Please let me know when would be a good time for you?

*This virtual dating is evidently done every day by lonely and/or devious individuals. When finding out something about the potential date, it is quite apparent the other person could be lying about their identity. It is impossible to know the intention of the other; one can come to know they are not telling the whole truth about themselves. In fact, the whole truth cannot be conveyed. Only a fictive relationship can be created.*

What are relationships for? They are for communication and community, which are the contexts for transformation. What do relationships require? Visual, auditory, tactile, cognitive, emotional, and spiritual aspects of a life together are the requirements for healthy relationships. What do relationships look like? Representation is today's measure of interpretation in this matter. The content of one's life is digital information on a screen. The way one performs life on an individual basis consigns each of us to interpret each other through social isolation. It is dissonant, the way one is supposed to balance isolation with pretending to be social.

Western culture has ingrained in people the notion that the person is cognizant and in control of their own cognitive destinies. The Cartesian model doubts all senses except the mind and what a person is thinking; hence Descartes iterates the words "I think, therefore I am." As Drew Leder has stated, "It is only because the body has intrinsic tendencies toward self-concealment could such tendencies be exaggerated by linguistic and technological extensions."[1] In other words, why is the Cartesian model, with its dualism and absence and alienation of the body, so persuasive to many? My explanation would be similar to the words of Martha Stout: "as a result of our histories, and of our inborn disposition to become dissociative when our minds need protection, moderately dissociated awareness is the normal mental status of all adult human beings."[2] This may be why so many think the way they live is best described by the Cartesian model. Persons existing within such a modality of thinking do so without considering their bodies.

Descartes leaves no room in this particular statement for the body. The physiology of the person is often manipulated with medication, and often with the intent to change cognitive processes. Agents are available to alter the person's awareness of particular problematic thinking. Substances are used and abused for recreational purposes as well. Body chemistry is so connected to relationships that this chemistry, when given other chemicals, can destroy personalities and families. Of course with all this internet reality, virtual as it is, there is internet sex, which feeds from internet seduction fantasy and internet relationships. No worry though, there is internet counseling.

Virtual relationships are about as personal as getting a text and an adrenaline chemical boost from that exchange of information. The lure may be the content of the connection; however, I contend it is the very process of fusion that secures these affairs and the content is only ancillary to engagement by the fusion process. The seduced becomes reduced to an object in media relations. The same is true of the many that spend hours playing video games, internet games, engaging with social media, or watching television. The subjective experience of the person is subverted by the intense feelings gained from interaction with media; there is a way to address this as an addictive force in the person's life. But it is more than that; media subversion of the subject makes for a more complete understanding of the process and ramifications of this affair.

1. Leder, *Absent Body*, 3.
2. Stout, *Myth of Sanity*, 104.

The most social some persons get these days is through social media. Is that even real relationship or community? These kinds of relationships are self-serving. Steve Pavlina states: "The notion that we are completely separate from everyone else is merely an illusion. Think of your relationships as external projections of the real you."[3] I agree with this partially, but contend there are others whom a person is in relation to and has relationships with that are more than just projections. Certainly there is interpretation of the other's behavior, but the other has acted and therefore can and is perceived. That perception is dependent on the action of the other, as a bodily being.

When one uses information-processing models to explain larger and larger slices of behavior, they seem compelled to isolate as their core something they can think of as being beyond information. The Cartesian model is flawed in that the body of the self and the other ought not to be left out of the equation. This contention preserves the other's bodily and soulful experience and behavior. In reaction to this lack of interactivity, there seems to be something very amiss; there is the need for the whole person to be involved in relationships. This is mostly achieved through communal interaction or through ritual.

It seems the idea of a virtual relationship without a bodily manifestation is a pseudo-relationship, not a relationship in actuality. Internet relationships exist as virtual and as concoctions of media over will. The key here is that virtual relationships are not real relationships. Virtual relationships are poorly constructed, unlike real relationships, which have the nuances of social reciprocity and social cues, or bodily cues. The bodily experience and/or the subject are excised from one another within virtual relationships. Regardless of the relationships that are made on the internet, a large amount of them are made with virtually no real knowledge of the individuals engaging in this interaction. Many people make these virtual relationships while they spend their time in isolation. This

---

3. Pavlina, *Personal Development*, 59.

loneliness is indeed the realer than real that Massumi has written about.[4] A friend is a friend indeed but not bodily, only virtually.

The disastrous thing is these pseudo-relationships seem realer than real, realer than everyday, real-life human relationships. The preference is not for the existential relationship lived in the world, but rather the virtual relationship, lived in the fusion process. Virtual processes replace ritual understandings and familial connections. Some people might forsake their actual relationships in the real world in favor of the virtual world. The process leaves one destitute and bereft of meaning. This leads many into isolation; often young adults end up in the basements of their parents houses suffering from a dissonance between their online friendship or relationship building and the real anger, loneliness, or depression experienced when one is cut off from real life and the real world.

What is the actual nature of human identities and relationships? Do they simultaneously include verbal, visual, auditory, and tactile dimensions? What kind of relationship is practical and what kind is not? One would think that the notion of relationship would need qualifiers or requisites. A real relationship requires cognitive, emotional, and tactile/kinesthetic components. One qualification for relationship is communication; other qualifications are based on the senses. Media process expects only two phenomena in order to operate on us: vision and hearing. The other senses are eliminated from communication and relationship in fusion. As Maxine Sheets-Johnstone has illustrated, the West (and for that matter, the whole world) is so "mesmerized by vision" that the real emotion-feeling body has been neglected.[5]

Every communicative relationship has content and process: what is said and how it is stated. Communicative relations involve reciprocity, either intentional or implied. There is no way not to communicate when one meets another in actuality. Even so, there is a measure of interpretation in relationships. Human relationships involve nonverbal communication as observed through bodily position, proximity, and gestures. Also, communication often includes

4. Massumi, "Realer than Real," 87.

5. Sheets-Johnstone, *Roots of Power*, 13.

behavior and observable actions. In fact, as soulful and/or bodily beings, there is no way to avoid communicating when interacting in a real-life social situation. A facial or bodily expression is always perceived by the other, whether in a relationship or not. The person is forever in relation to others and has an affective dimension.

One could ask: Why are real relationships not easy? Media make it easy to avoid the hard stuff, and what is forgotten is how to do what it takes to sustain a real relationship. Many have forgotten or have never learned to read social cues. Baudrillard suggests "media are not producers of socialization, but of exactly the opposite, of the implosion of the social in the masses."[6] In fact there is a way of desocialization that is creating a *culture of autism*. Simple communication induces so much anxiety that one becomes either isolative or socially phobic. People read social cues and expression; the social cues are the most affected in a detrimental way through fusion, because there is no way to have a full human interaction without a person recognizing these cues. These cues are social in nature; therefore, social cues involve full interaction in a social space.

In such a social space there is a duality implied, not a single voice (univocal), but a dialectical moment created for the two voices involved. This, however, is impossible by the sheer fact that one cannot know the nature of the individual they are communicating with; one is simply caught up in a fusion process. This fusion occurs and media drives the desire and intentionality of the conversation or messaging. No eye-to-eye contact, no body, no body language, no social cues: there are only text and screen. The Turing test demonstrates the slight difference between the communication of sentient beings and that of machines (computers). When one is on the internet chatting with another, they may not know with whom or with what they are communicating, because all of their senses are not engaged. This phenomenological situation implies one can no less know the other, nor the supposed intent of the other, which is in fact no other at all, but one's desire for another.

Relationships involve contingencies; virtual relationships take away this relative dimension. Relationships between persons

6. Baudrillard, *Simulacra and Simulation*, 81.

involves dependency, but this is not so for virtual relationships. In the thinking of the American philosopher Richard Rorty, everything is contingency and relativity.[7] In virtual reality there is no contingency, only process. In the virtual there is nothing that has relationship with anything else. This is because everything in the fusion process has become one with the process. In the process there are no distinctions. If everything is contingent, then a person's existence is contingent upon something or someone else. It is evident persons are undefined until they enter a relationship with another; in this vein, it is not likely that one is defined by a machine (i.e., an interaction with a computer is machine-like). Therefore, human relationships are based on communication, bodily reality or tangibility, and expression. This is not the case with machines. Media process defines what a person is and encapsulates the subject into this process. The subject becomes one with the process and is part of a violation that is beyond the control of the subject, as media violate the subject.

Relationships are about exposure and vulnerability as well as rooted in alienation, which starts with the split subject. The *alien* in the word *alienation* implies the nature of the subject and its other, which is both alien and foreign. The conscious and unconscious worlds are troubled by this fusing of entities into the one process. The subject is split between the conscious and the unconscious; this causes alienation and vulnerability. Evans expresses it this way: "The subject is fundamentally split, alienated from himself, and there is no escape from this division, no possibility of 'wholeness' or synthesis."[8] The fusion process of violation happens partly due to the fact that alienating is a significant factor for violation. Once the nature of the subject is exposed, then the way fusion happens to the subject becomes evident. The split allows the process to cross the two domains of the subjective life of the individual, both the conscious and the unconscious. This exposes the relationship each person has with media and with the other. The relationship one has with media is much like the relationship a person has with

---

7. Rorty, *Irony, Contingency, and Solidarity*, 187.

8. Evans, *Introductory Dictionary of Lacanian Psychoanalysis*, 9.

other people; if the subject is exposed enough, alienation is the result, making the conscious and the unconscious available to being ensnared. Vulnerability also speaks to the nature of relationship; once vulnerability is made apparent, it is easier to access the other's mind. If one loses oneself, one stands to gain a relationship more so than if a person preserves their inner world.

Relationships are at the heart of what it means to be a person of a nation, race, or ethnicity. At the heart of what it means to be in relationship is the conscious and unconscious world. Communion with the other comes with the admission of vulnerability. Relationships through the sharing of conscious and unconscious spaces, through communion and ritual, are made manifest in the richest and most meaningful ways. The most significant way to interact socially is through ritual, which can be as simple as a handshake and as complex as rolling out a red carpet; but this possibility is stripped away by the fusion process because it disallows physical and material manifestations of the will. Real communication is communion with others and is the place of transformation of the subject.

# 9

# Pixilated Personhood

*I have been viewing others' Facebook posts and it seems everyone has so much going on in their lives, from recording their children and pets to going to online events. I have so little to do. My friends I spend time gaming with all talk about how they are so great at games. I have to admit I am envious of the amount of stuff people have going on in their lives. I have little to post these days and I feel lonely. I would like to post more of who I am, but so many people get roasted for the things they post that are personal. I do not want others to know I am so unable to articulate my likes and desires online. My relationships have become toxic; I am freaking out all the time, others have said negative and insulting things to me online. I have been abused online. I feel like a martyr because I feel shunned.*

Some cognitive fallacies occur in the above description of an identity gone awry. 1) Facebook posts are not necessarily true or real. 2) People with whom one games are not all real friends, but rather are largely people met online. These friends are virtual. 3) There is the cognitive distortion equivalent to mind-reading—one reads the content and descriptions from online posts and believes they are real thoughts others have. Real toxicity is in the act of participating in an unknown world of the virtual.

One should understand the subject-media process and fusion scramble and mesmerize, with their flashes and glitter, mega-pixel domains going into territories, the places deep in the mind that program at the subliminal level, so that the subject becomes an object. This is indicative of the power at work through media. Fusion breaks down the unity of the self, the continuities, and divides it against itself. Žižek states: "Today, even the mass media are aware of the extent to which our perception of reality, including the reality of our innermost self-experience depends upon symbolic fictions. . ."[1] Twenty-first-century media entails more than just the internet, but through internet connectivity the subject is greatly affected and identity evaporates because a person may become anything they wish.

This particular medium provides access to avatar status, whereby self-definition is morphed from the inside out. Media give simple concrete ideas of what subjectivity is supposed to be for the person. Subjectivity is very complex and involves identification of the person with individuals on the screen. A person has trouble forming identity due to the barrage of new material and icons provided by media even in each moment. The flow and experience of subjectivity is conveniently objectified by way of, as Jose Luis Bermúdez et al. called them, "intuitions about the psychological continuities involved in the survival of a person but also with perhaps even more powerful intuitions about the necessary unity of a single subject's experiences."[2] The disparities and complications of subjectivity are complex, indefinite, and fluid; however, they are often represented as being simple and concrete in nature. The actuality of media is their ever-present overcoming of the person in such a way that all experience occurs in a fictive, media-constructed realm.

The work that has been done on the presentation of self addresses the roles people play in life much as in theatrical performance. This constructivist position has become the attitude of many in the westernized world. Ever since performativity theory and the constructivist point of view came into dominance in social theory, the self has been under the eye of criticism and manufacture. Social media exposes details about the person, thereby placing them under

1. Žižek, *Tarrying with the Negative*, 11.
2. Bermúdez et al., *Body and the Self*, 76.

the eye of criticism. The social cues that are elicited in the somatic (physical) body, the body language expressed, and the construction of the inner self are all a part of everyday life. But now, through the internet-oriented and constructed manner in which media creates identity, one is created through a perfect format. Through pixilation and modification, one believes they make themselves as an image: personalized, internet "I"conography.

The person can create identity in multiple ways and on many platforms or forums, but can only do so from the inside, and media have already planted that which one could represent oneself with: the identity given the subject by media. This is the approach of the meaning-making that occurs within media. The processing of information stored away in the deepest parts of the person's being come from imagery and the flirtations of media. Though one believes they are creating their own self, they are actually just producing the remnants of media they have been exposed to and are trapped in the fusion process or media process.

The self-making process each person experiences as they participate with the other is informed by the media process. There is no longer a self or even subject, but there is fusion. One becomes the process; the content of experience is constructed and even reconstructed. The significant way of knowing identity involves knowing who and what media make one out to be; the making of the self is not in the control of the subject, but is determined in the media process, which is fusion.

Internet emancipation is a process through which persons become active producers or cultural producers, expressing identities within the framework of what media have offered to that date. The opposite is true as well because asking, "Who am I?" and creating one's personal pages sets them free of content one would not like others to know. This is constructivism at work, making selves and meaning public without revealing true selves. Any time one says something significant, part of their message is always left out. In true Lacanian terms, it is surely the case that discourse is never able to communicate the entire truth. This is true of marketing because something about the product is inevitably left out. Therefore, any information put into representation is susceptible to omission of ideas. Also, the intention of the other is not known; therefore, deceit or inaccuracy can result. Given the nature of the digital and graphic space, one is limited by imagery, whereby words could more accurately convey the matter to be communicated. However, it must be kept in mind that even language is suspect when it comes to representing a matter because the full truth cannot be told.

The matter of social justice provides a challenge here as well. When one considers Carol Hanisch's idea that "the personal is political,"[3] this notion of justice reaches some turbulence because if the person is constructed, then the creative moment leaves room for interpretation. This interpretation is subject to scrutiny, and then the political work is compromised. Personal life becomes politicized, and the voice of media reaches far into the person's psyche to create identity. Identity politics is complicated because any time a group of people is represented, some piece of data is potentially omitted. An injustice occurs because the whole of the group is not sufficiently presented in media; the whole truth cannot be known. Media's virtual identities and bodies are encrypted with messages from the particular source of media. The univocal verifies the perception of identity, and though there seem to be many voices, the singular voice is echoed in the internet identity. A minority who does not fit media representation becomes completely excluded. Not every voice within the minority group is heard because only one can be represented. This is an example of the univocal phenomenon.

When discussing identity within relationships, one may consider trying to categorize actual self, being, or identity. In all relationships and identities there is consideration of a power differential. The way the West has traditionally understood power is to couch it in dichotomous thinking. Western ideology uses dichotomous thought in order to separate, divide, and supersede the other in order to capture or maintain a position of power. Media use representation of correlates or dichotomies to manipulate, victimize, and injure public bodies in political spaces. According to Sheets-Johnstone, "intersubjectivity (the relationship of subjects) rather than inter-corporeality (the relationship between bodies)

3. Hanisch, "Personal is Political," 1.

constitutes the conceptual point of departure for understanding socio-political relations."[4] The flux of existence is difficult to communicate; dualistic thought does not capture the flow of it. Also, the tendency to objectify something which is other, making it less important or marginal, is a strategy to preserve the subject. Since the subject is the center of philosophical speculation, the other is often understood as living in a separate and minimal state and as if the other is of little consequence. Those who live as other, or of difference, are labeled, described, or objectified, are stigmatized by a conceptualization that does not truly capture their lived experience. Social justice identity politics puts individuals and groups at odds with each other and creates us-versus-them scenarios.

As media presents the other it can only be represented in a limited way; the full truth cannot be told. Hence, certain important questions arise: Exactly what is one compromising in the encounter of person and media? What is this identity which is compromised? The whole person, as inner subjectivity and corporeality, is subverted. In Lacanian thought the person is formed through the "mirror stage."[5] This formation of the person happens in the identification with the "specular image."[6] The person can see themselves in a mirror and the specular image is that which appears in the mirror as both oneself and other. The experience of continuity involves the perception of identification with the specular image over time. This is where the person draws conclusions about their identity.

Fusion involves a very similar action, whereby the specular image appears on the screen. In this scenario there is less control within the process of identification. The person sees themselves on the screen and the virtual image is that which appears on the screen as both oneself and the other. The screen is where the person identifies in a way that is out of the person's control. As media gets into the workings of one's cognitive processing and executive functioning, as a subject-media process, the functions of media are enticement, entrapment, and obliteration of the person's singularity

4. Sheets-Johnstone, *Roots of Power*, 59.

5. Evans, *Introductory Dictionary of Lacanian Psychoanalysis*, 117.

6. Evans, *Introductory Dictionary of Lacanian Psychoanalysis*, 193.

and center of being. The imaginary or fictive nature of the virtual image as singular is very deceptive. The fusion process lures the person toward identities that change rapidly in media process and its representations. Media have a profound affect not just on subjective experience of mind, but also on the somatic tactile-kinesthetic experience; the body is transformed and subsumed by the identification processes in fusion. Compromise in integrity occurs with the communication of identity as internet identity or virtual identity.

In the process of fusion, the body is created just as any other social construct, except by media and not by the body's presumed proprietor, the person. Media manipulates the perception of somatic bodies. The person becomes disconnected from their physical body as they gaze at the screen. This is reminiscent of the Lacanian concept of the mirror stage. This mirroring is equivocated in media as one experiences the expression of the body on the screen. In the experiential world the subjective body could possibly be experienced by the individual, but in actuality, this body numbs and falls away as one is soaked in media. No longer can one define themselves because they are defined within media and its devices. The person is driven by media to accede to its control; media takes over as the body of media, that manifestation of all bodies. When turning to the body of media, the fusion of bodies is the folding into the subject-media process. The body of media is the whole of all virtual bodies and the way media expects them to be, whether thin and metro or some other formulation concocted by media. Fusion happens and the subjective body becomes nonexperienced, but rather experienced as the virtual body. There is no escape from this, to the extent that all subjects become the body of media.

There is no reality outside of or beyond the perspective of media to determine sex, mores, sexuality, or especially body image. Giving the body its own determination turns into being overcome and converted to the relational and mesmerizing fusion process. The subjective body experience is manipulated by the screen, when one believes consuming a given product facilitates the experience of a different body. Desire and seduction take on new meanings as images of beauty are indefinable and yet defined by media. Through the subject-media process the catchy jingles have invaded personal lives, making things like sex public, not private, matters. The frenzy of ads about substances for consumers can be catchy and mesmerizing within the body of media. These lay waste the notion that beauty is in the eye of the beholder. Beauty is in the eye of media, which is a determined effect of the subject-media process. The appendages of the virtual body are plastered all over magazines and internet, on the news media and prime time television and with extensive commercialization. In a sense one is creating new bodies every second of existence. The body creates new bodies in an endless flow of disaster after catastrophe, and collision of the virtual with the real. Bodies are no longer lived, but virtualized through fusion. These bodies are captive in the subject-media process and through virtual determination become the body of media.

The body of the subject-media process presents as an unattainable beauty which conveys the strongest and most humiliating dissonances; it is lavishly adorned, embellished, and emaciated. With the loss of insight into the very physical body of being, the masses pursue perfection through the virtual or media available to a stricken population. All is lost in the expectations of persons seeking the body's perfection as the body of media, the heavenly, the diva. It seems as though being caught in the whirlwind of the subject-media process's expectations causes such a dissonance that the hatred of the body physical develops as the body of media becomes manifest. The body of media's image creates one's disgust with one's own fleshly body.

The body is of utmost magnitude for the individual, who is forced to recreate. For example, body hedonism is an issue that traces its way to exercise, dieting, and instilling in the masses what the body needs. This healthy lifestyle is a motivator for many who have been seduced by media. Exercise is pushed beyond the realm of health into the depravity of bondage, to the search for another body, to the angelic. Bodies are constructed by the subject-media process through which persons stay engaged within the virtual body; the desired body can never be completely reached.

Media seduce the masses with perfect images, asserting that the body must be very thin, which becomes a curse to those who do not follow this rule. The subject-media process may seek the altering of one's appearance, even by suggesting the use of a scalpel or laser. Persons have as their focus representations which often stray away from the medical model in pursuit of a perfect body, the *virtual* body. This body exists in the actuality of media and is derived from the body of media and becomes the consumer body as well.

Where the subject-media process represents the body of media, the bodies defined by media may not be equivalent to the way a person experiences their body, and therefore the person feels the need to modify their body. The consumer body brings forth worldwide appeal, products of wellness nomenclature, which are all at once approved by certain entities for their safety and effectiveness. The line between use and abuse is rarely a strict demarcation that lets the body know when to curb its appetite and to use the treatments of marketed value. Any limitation of the body's potential for modification is the evil which is abhorred by consumers, for they do not want to learn the actual outcome of the use of any product, but rather want to remain focused on the desired outcome.

Since bodies drop away and persons become virtual bodies, they are not constructed in reality; the person experiences them in the virtual sense, and much differently. The virtual body is an avatar that one thinks they construct, but is instead constructed by media. No one is able to have the sensations once known to bodies of flesh; instead, people vibrate, dissociate, and live literally as the screen of cinema, television, social media, and the internet. As a result, the body of media takes over perception. Persons are not extensions of the body of media, but are the body of media, meaning they live as that which exists on the screen. The body is completely identified with media's representation to the extent that one's body is the body on the screen and thus has become a media representation absolutely; this experience of fusion is the virtual body. The body of the screen and the virtual body are identical; there is no more subjective experience of one's own separate body. This is much stronger than enmeshment with media, but involves the transformation of the body into the virtual body. When one dresses in a particular style, that person is dressing the virtual body. The person has no experience of the lived body, but rather they are a performative production of the subject-media process.

# 10

# Global Greatness

*"I'D LIKE TO TEACH the world to sing in perfect harmony." This is the jingle from a cola ad I heard as a child and remember to this day. It was the "I have a dream" of my generation. The idea of the whole world coming together in a nonapocalyptic moment seemed like the best idea going. It was more than coexisting; it was total participation in oneness and in harmony. I remember listening to "Do the Locomotion" and the Coca-Cola jingle while my 3rd grade class did calisthenics. Nowadays, it seems like everyone knows everyone's business. With social media there is no escape from the way in which one's life is exposed to the world. The world, not just a village, is raising our next generation, and it seems to do more harm than good. Who put this in place? How am I responsible for the conditions people are exposed to throughout the world? Are we just one global dysfunctional family?*

In fusion the person becomes a mere connection. With the notion of connection I allude to Deleuze's concept of desire connecting to desire. Fusion is a violation, a subjugating force, and a marriage by communication that violates and entraps any possibility of control in the world for individuals. Baudrillard states: "the masses respond with ambivalence, to deterrence they respond with disaffection, or with an always enigmatic belief."[1] With the subject-media process there is a weaker response by the masses; there is

1. Baudrillard, *Simulacra and Simulation*, 81.

a complete annihilation of any psychological property they have brought to the process. The subject-media process is a violent marriage in which the masses have absolutely no control or influence; it is in fact a process of enslavement. The subject-media process occurs in tandem with the globalization of the entire earth. These are phenomenological forces which have hit the world, in tandem, and which wipe away all boundaries and differences. If there is no contrasting culture, no hybridity, no difference, and all people play and ritualize the same way, then it is by subject-media process. Differences are helpful to a world that seeks to unify on common grounds; without differences there is no basis for comparison.

Due to the subject-media process, the world has fewer and fewer media events that do not saturate and corrupt the world and its people with distorted views of reality. Each event has many spins and agendas that, in knowing, it must realize there is no truth nor is there a real to be found. This process either strips the masses of a firm grip on reality, soaking them with lies, or turns many people into cynics, which it seems to be aimed at doing. It is no wonder conspiracy theorists abound. Nonetheless, these theorists are caught in the subject-media process as well. The most intellectual persons may be particularly proud of their empirical skills, but the fraud and flood of certain ideations, feelings, and sensations the subject-media process produces overwhelms them. Subject-media process is a large-scale rendering of fusion in the individual subject's experience. Fusion is a bonding, magnetic, and disarming process; the subject-media process is the formation of events that flood the world with media happenings, colloquially known as narrative moments.

With globalization the world's population is becoming terribly confused, fragmented, and disparate. It is not only the interaction with media that is at issue here. The world is witnessing a phenomenon that eats up modes of thinking and devours them by use of force through auditory and visual senses. Nothing makes it into this processual field without being distorted. Truth may not gain any meaning at all when handled by this meaning-making and suppressive force. As the partner of globalization, media play more of a role than politics. This tandem of forces, media and globalization, can

propel respected and distinguished individuals into the gloomy un-
derworld of tabloid miscarriage. On a worldwide scale, one's fame
or shame can be sensationalized by the forces of globalizing and
media-driven pronunciations. There is no caution taken by anyone.
Forces go on sweeping the globe with astounding perpetual effect;
hence globalization and subject-media process work hand-in-hand
to affect the world.

There may be no escape from the ideas and notions of this tandem's meaning-making, this world-distorting witness to trivial and
provocative people and issues. The effect of this tandem is to both
gain the dependence of individuals and to decentralize thinking, as
such decentralizing effects a disorganization or disorientation of the
masses. The forces do not work together to brainwash anyone, but
rather to appeal to the senses and contain persons within a skewed
view of the world, replacing any type of worldview. There is no
common theme except perhaps that of consumerism. The tandem
of globalization and aggressive decentering by the subject-media
process is not swaying the world toward any economic system, so
as to put a template on the face of the socioeconomics of the world.
The value of items a consumer can obtain is surely exponentially
multiplied by the variety of choices there are, and that variety is
quite baffling. This disparity of choice is not necessarily a freedom
or some kind of controlling apparatus, but rather a meddling or
confusion. There may be those who see strength in diversity, but
this is not the issue here. With the multiplicity of choices the world
has to offer in terms of consumption, it leaves standing institutions staggered by a plethora, and proliferating number, of ideas.
The subject-media process has no aim, not even novelty or fit; it
just offers a frame and reframe for a confounded world population.
Hence, fusion is important for facilitating this process. Without fusing to the variety of flashes and images, a consumer would not be
lost in this decentering parade of images and ideas. The consumer
has no choice in the matter because of the grafting of idea to desire
in the fusion process.

The process of the tandem also scours the intellectual and aca-
demic scenes by offering unfiltered and unlimited knowledge. Accuracy is not an aim and nor is censorship; there is plenty of blame

to go around, but no one to pin it on. One cannot state accurately where the responsibility lies for the excess of violence that fills campuses in many forms. There seems to be plenty of action and little learning. Individuals and populations are swayed by fusion and the subject-media process. This is not to say the mass absorbs the individual but rather to say both the masses and the individual are captured by a subject-media process. There is a synergistic affair with the populace down to the very singular person, between the medium and the persons, between media and the masses.

The subject-media process is not so focused on the postmodern concern of overproduction of signs, the grandiose nature of media designs, or the "implosion of meaning"[2] as Baudrillard has called it. *The concern, rather, is with how media uses a process of exposure and its mesmerizing effect to engage societies in enculturation.* The key here is the understanding of media concentrates on process and media effects in postmodern times, not just the signs and significations media produces. *This process is significantly related to the process that ritual life had within societies in previous and ancient times.* Meaning-making continues over and over through media, with its flashes of imagery and its pixilation. The subject-media process coalesces upon and engulfs the world. The global technological environment is characterized by a loss of contact with basic assumptions about selves and the material tactile world. Something is missing in a world of the virtual and image. Has a world of technocrats in the twenty-first century lost its soul in the shadow of virtual realities? William Barrett once asked a related question: "What shall it profit a whole civilization, or culture, if it gains knowledge and power over the material world, but loses any adequate idea of the conscious mind, the human self, at the center of all that power?"[3]

Deleuze utilizes the concept of desiring-machines when formulating an understanding of private and collective, as well as unconscious and conscious activity. In the case of fusion, desire for connectivity and the impulse for fake meaning result in

2. Baudrillard, *Simulacra and Simulation*, 31.
3. Barrett, *Death of the Soul*, 166.

the internalization of the meaning-making machine: the screen. Production of desire is in the fields of the psyche and the socius; production of desire is an exciting adventure, where desire meets desire. But, like the flits and flashes of imagery presented by the global, desire quickly passes. Representation becomes the real which culture desires. Even more so, culture engineers myths to structure the real into representation. Ads are only representations manifest for the virtual, only momentarily quenching desire. In the present state of affairs on earth, theorists are formulating a global story. Globalization is a real and homologous hegemony making universalization and multiculturalism extinct. Multicultural stories lack substance for those who are left in the wake of globalization and the subject-media process. The multicultural becomes a homogeneous product appearing as a singularity.

There may be noncompliance by persons or attempted revolt against the effects of media, but it is quite certain that once exposed to media, persons are fused to their processes. With the mechanistic connection of media to the psyches of the global citizens, each person comes to think like all the others. In understanding Deleuze's theory of the univocal it must be understood that a Marxian or Hegelian dialectic is superseded. Deleuze questions: "what does the dialectician himself want? What does this will which wills the dialectic want? It is an exhausted force which does not have the strength to affirm a difference, a force which no longer acts but reacts to the forces that dominate it . . ."[4] Given the nature of dialectic, it is overpowered by global oneness and falters at any attempt to offer an opposition to this univocal phenomenon called globalization. Therefore, with some discrepancies, it can be stated that Baudrillard collapsed the dichotomous by entertaining the notion that globalization is univocal.

Media have not put the whole world economically, culturally, or personally at odds and have not really given every faction and persona a voice; though there seem to be multiple voices and options, the masses are at the dictate of media production. The presumed individualism that comes with globalization, along with

---

4. Deleuze, *Nietzsche and Philosophy*, 9.

more advances in knowledge for the marginalized, actually is a limiting force in the world. Idols, figures, nations, and commodities are all swallowed up by global consumerism. Splinter-groups, factions, and terrorists cannot stop globalization, for they are only reflections of its fractal nature. Devastation and destruction have been pounded into us time after time by media that record each sickening sight as a spectacle, or rather just another media event. With globalization, media have no shame; terror is commonplace, even expected. Media violence is more than virtual; there are real victims, but they are represented by media as images. During the horrific experience of 9/11 there were victims, but at the time of the event media played video over and over around the world. The realer than real touched something deeper within us, perhaps subconsciously but more often flagrantly in the open. 9/11 was an event with no possible dialectic to explain it. Many were lost, but the media sensationalized the event by focusing on destruction at the very time of the contemptuous act; videos of destruction played in our faces in a sickening loop. Meaning-making in this world is done by media, and there is no mistake the masses honor terror and horror. Media turn horror into something benign, yet this seems to be the expectation. In the present world culture, the masses invite, without trembling, the most horrific imagery possible. Again, this horrific and heinous act took the lives of many and should never be minimized in moral or political thought.

Baudrillard argues "the moral condemnation and the holy alliance against terrorism are on the same scale as the prodigious jubilation at seeing this global superpower destroyed."[5] This is how the terrorists would understand it. Baudrillard also identifies it as the "terroristic imagination which dwells in all of us."[6] This is a strong statement, indicting all persons with such a grim and sinister approach toward the other. Baudrillard paints a dim view of persons when he mentions "what stays with us, above all else, is the sight of the images. This impact of the images, and their fascination, are necessarily what we retain, since images are, whether

5. Baudrillard, *Screened Out*, 4.
6. Baudrillard, *Screened Out*, 5.

we like it or not, our primal scene."[7] Baudrillard has written about
the obscenity, spectacle, and virtuality of horrifying events, often
from a staunch position of neutrality or even pessimism. It should
be noted media are what advances such thoughts of horror within
the consciousness of persons. Baudrillard also observes the 9/11
attacks "radicalized the relation of the image to reality."[8] These images will have renunciation in the cumulative psyche of Americans
and others around the world. The theme of Baudrillard's work, that
globalization is at war with itself, is telling of the univocity and the
world being beyond the dialectic. The world is developing in one
voice, not through opposing voices of thesis and antithesis. Two
points which synthesize, the thesis and the antithesis, are actually
not manifested in the subject-media process. Oneness of the world
and its immediacy to the population is induced by media exposure;
the violence it does to the masses and the individual is devastating.

In the wake of disaster the world still lusts for violence. Just
watch prime time television. Though nothing in it exists, *ipso facto*,
everything is in virtual happenings. This was absolutely Baudrillard's conviction; violence is at once promoted as virtual and thus
more real. Unlike universalism, which recognizes otherness, globalization minimizes multiculturalism and difference in favor of
the dissonance pronounced in the name of oneness and violence.
People and violence are pixilated into bytes of information projected
perfectly on a screen that is determined by the global. There is a
proof that there is only one dimension to globalization. A globalized
world may pose challenges for anarchy because of the oneness of its
voice. That oneness overshadows possibilities for those who would
not conform to the rule of global normativity. The univocal that
Deleuze and Baudrillard have conceptualized, which designates the
microcosmic and the macrocosmic (meaning the global), is spelled
out clearly and is difficult to contest. As a sociological phenomenon,
globalization is a unifying hegemony that includes all categories of
life and assimilates all peoples of the world through consumption;
it is not just nominally the consumption of the person via fusion.

7. Baudrillard, *Screened Out*, 26.
8. Baudrillard, *Screened Out*, 27.

Oppositional groups and political revolutions may rise up within localities. However, none can come from outside of globalization. In a one-world understanding, with all the technology involved in wars, computer screens make war *un*real, virtual, and then realer than real. This is the conclusion and fulfillment of desire within the subject-media process and globalization.

There is some question regarding the degree to which globalization has affected indigenous cultures. Many communities and homes in up-and-coming countries have the same technology as the rest of the world and have become part of the transformation. Žižek states: "The class problematic of workers' exploitation is (transformed) into the multiculturalist problematic of the 'intolerance of Otherness.'"[9] In the postpolitical world, the globalized world, these fractures of difference and otherness have surfaced as problems that are practically divisive. For Baudrillard it is no longer possible to overturn globalization through some dichotomous worldview. The virtual is reality and sustains the status quo, and the struggle between classes is dampened the more technology trickles into many communities throughout the world; this is progress. The world has rapidly moved to realizing the idea of global village as commonalities in terms of economic aspirations and technological progress have been emphasized by politicians and opinion makers, more than differences such as religion, culture, and ethnicity. Globalization of the world is the ultimate celebration of the political, economic, and social homogenization of the global population.

Derrida invited the deconstruction and the demise of the relevance of man, and the subject.[10] Through deconstruction all history, ethics, and mores are subject to dismissal, revision, and fragmentation processes that destroy their continuity, leaving all persons of history open to criticism and reevaluation. The demythologizing media makes an impression on the masses. Persons that seem to have made a difference in history are swallowed up by the body of media, where differentiation ceases. There is the folding together of all persons, no matter how different they are in terms of culture

9. Žižek, *Fragile Absolute*, 10.

10. Derrida, *Margins of Philosophy*, 119.

and outlook. The body of media consolidates all differences. Media transforms disparities and differences in the world into one global movement in the direction of oneness and certainly proves to be centered on the univocal. Idealisms such as multiculturalism are interpreted by media, and the subject is informed by these interpretations. Thousands of ideas, images, and voices flash before the subject as it is melded with them.

Robert Ellwood stated: "The modern world. . .is often alienating and dehumanizing, denying people easy access to the depths of their souls. Myth, like all great literature, can become universal, transcending particular cultural settings to provide general models of the human predicament and the way out of it."[11] The myths produced by machines are well received into the global topology, where blog machines are all ready to be connected with other blog machines. The myth of the machine, the machine of the myth, machines connecting to machines, myths allegorizing myths: all is at play in a nondual, univocal, and global economy of meaning. Nothing remains hidden here; media are everywhere to know, to be the world of ever-turning drama, disaster, and moral decay.

Desire, in the postmodern global psychological milieu, is set up in mythologies reminiscent of a young Romanticism which budded in Europe to meet the desires of the aesthetic experience of the time. The desire that presently affects the world develops out of artificial meaning and resonates in the digitized minds of those who seek its fulfillment. Ritual and myth are not underscored; these two phenomena are replaced with media, media devices, or meaning-making machines which create digital meaning for the modern mind. Imagery, icons, and sound bytes advance a totalizing experience; at the same time there is a tantalization in the pursuit of trends and ways of being represented by the body of media. The obscene obsessions of the creators' magic flashes of light and images seem to invade even private lives and the myths they possess. Obscene it is when one's ethics and mores are acquired from a flickering screen.

11. Ellwood, *Politics of Myth*, 177.

# 11

# Real Ritual: Reprise

*THE CHURCH ANYMORE IS no longer meeting my needs physically, emotionally, or mentally, much less spiritually. The thing I am most discouraged about is the spiritual aspect. It used to be spirituality was couched nicely in ritual and relationship. Now it seems everyone goes their own way. Church has become so geared to the individual and commercialization, having its interest now in numbers. While mega-churches are on the rise, communal spiritual engagement is limited. There is so much fanfare that church sometimes seems like a play or concert where each person sits in their own bubble and enjoys the gratifying experience, and each person is self-aggrandizing as well. Humility among a community of believers seems harder to come by in the twenty-first century. While I avoid the smaller churches that seem akin to Mom-n-Pop stores because they lack structure, and relationships often involve so much infighting, I long for a church that realizes the importance of relationship and ritual through communing together.*

Fusion is the process whereby a person's subjective experience is influenced heavily, violated, and ultimately stolen by experience with media. This process happens on both conscious and unconscious levels. Because the subject or person is characterized by intrinsic weakness, the fusion process is guaranteed to happen to anyone exposed to media. In reality there is no way to escape media in Western culture. The Westerner is born into media, with the nature of Western society's exposure to it. For infants in the West, exposure to media happens immediately upon birth and even prior to birth. The seductive nature of media process or fusion is ineluctable; persons are swimming in media all the time and unaware of it as well. This being the case, it is important to know what processes fusion has replaced. It must be understood that both for the individual and for the masses, fusion and the subject-media process replace the functions of ritual.

Media replaces ritual through the process of the subjective interaction the person has with media. The meaning-making space ritual has played in the life of the individual and the masses has been overtaken by the subject-media process. Participation in ritual, both individual and communal, takes time and practice. When considering the ritual process, there is a sort of transpersonal event that engages the participant. This happens in many performative acts within ritual space. There are situations where the person is transcended or the individual reaches a union with an Other; neither the person nor the process is compromised. Ritual runs as deep as real love. Arpad Szakolczai carefully discusses the coming together of lovers by stating "it is not the 'I' that loves the 'you'; rather it is the 'it', the love itself that emerges in the 'in-between' of two human beings [sic], forming and transforming both, by creating a single unit that cannot be separated without a tragedy; a kind of 'death.'"[1] The implication here for the understanding of the in-betweenness is that of process being the focus, rather than adhesion or some sort of connection. The subject and media come into interaction in process; it is not the subject that attaches to media, though there is subversion by media. In the process of subversion, there is a sort of apeiron, a quality of nonbinary flux, which causes the subject to gravitate toward and be enamored with media. This process is neither dialectic nor tripartite, but just exists as would the blooming of a flower.

Dennis W. Rook observes that "ritual experience is built around an episodic string of events . . . Ritual action is designed

1. Szakolczai, "Liminality and Experience," 158.

to conform to stereotyped scripts, and acting in conformity with a prescribed script is considered to be intrinsically rewarding."[2] Specific media activities and events are structured in a linear fashion whereby the same routine is demonstrated over and over again, over periods of time, and follows scripts that are significant to those who participate, willingly or unwittingly, with the process. The subject-media process does not include unintentional moves, but quite necessarily presents the masses with a sense of purpose or belonging. Media provide that which is necessary to continue to live in a media-filled world. Media provide process and content for persons to engage in meaning-making. The underlying idea is there is no meaning unless it is made.

Construction of reality in the minds of many, through representation and process, is how meaning is made. In ritual there is transformative power and a structuring of the way persons experience and think about life. Media have within them the same transformative power. Bruce Kapferer states what he focuses on is "ritual dynamics as a structuration of perception and of cognition in which particular human potentialities both of experience and of meaningful construction may be formed."[3] Nonetheless, Kapferer understands the potential of ritual is a "thoroughgoing reality of its own."[4] The truth of this statement is found in the levels of transformation ritual brings to particular lives and nations. Kapferer credits Victor Turner for presenting ritual as the "basis for the development of a general cultural, social, and political theory. In his vision, this was all the more so because he understood ritual formations worldwide as embedding the grounded and fundamental ingredients of human symbolic construction and their enduring paradoxes."[5] Turner looks at the process of ritual and the representations it produces.

The fusion process happens to change the corresponding representation of the cultural, social, and political within the framework of the individual's experience. The virtual, in the sense of

2. Rook, "Ritual Dimension," 252.
3. Kapferer, "Ritual Dynamics," 37.
4. Kapferer, "Ritual Dynamics," 37.
5. Kapferer, "Ritual Dynamics," 38.

media representations, has replaced the potential ritual possessed to exponentially change lives. This change is facilitated through the multitude of representations which exist in virtual spaces within the world of media. Meaning in the media world entertains the person in order to ensnare the subject in a process by the devices of the particular medium. Subject-media process has an enormous impact upon the masses and is to be understood as the replacement for the high ritual performed by large groups and populations of the world. Kapferer suggests, "With social and political processes of demythologization and the gathering secularism associated with modernization and globalization, the dynamics of rite are not likely to have such ramifying effects (new political and economic formation) through social and political space."[6] Ritual has been demythologized, modernized, and globalized.

Media are largely composed of demythologized or empty content which has little to do with the meaning-making; it is content and process through which meaning takes hold and hence the power of the subject-media process. However, process is where one returns to find meaning in the investigation of ritual and media. One is able to discuss going beyond representation and meaning in order to identify the dynamics or processes of ritual. As has been attested by Kapferer's work, that which envelops the subject is the process of ritual. Therefore media grasp the person through a weakened subject, an alienated subject, or as is derived from Lacan, the split subject. Nic Beech discusses the ritual process and its power in liminality, which is the state of uncertainty or perplexity that happens in the middle stage of a ritual, when partakers of the ritual precede the conversion to the place of understanding at the end of the ritual.[7] Beech states that in "liminality, in which the ritual subject or 'liminar' is ambiguous and passes through a realm that has few or none of the attributes of the 'before' and 'after' states; and aggregation, the consummation of the passage. At this stage, the liminar has reached a new identity position and they are expected

---

6. Kapferer, "Ritual Dynamics," 45.

7. Beech, "Liminality and the Practices of Identity Reconstruction," 3.

to adopt certain norms."[8] The weakness in the stage of liminality through which the person proceeds demonstrates the power of ritual to morph a being from one state to another. This power relationship also expresses itself in media process, which also activates the sculpting of identity.

Ritual is redefined by media process, and the experience of media transforms the person and their physicality much in the way ritual has for centuries. The person is transported to a different and intensified level of meaning-making experience, which is characterized by the ceaseless pattern of changing representations. The person's body takes on the markings of media exchange and becomes a partaker in the liminal space of decibels and frequencies; the person never fully emerges from that state or trance. Ultimately, life has become stagnant as persons slump ceaselessly and unadventurously in front of their TV or PC monitors. The requirement of living life with one's body, in one's body, or as one's body, has become unnecessary in the very nature of media itself.

The life of the body, the social body, becomes the body of media; this is the masses' experience of the screen in the subject-media process. Rook observes that in ritual life the "natural body and social body reacted on each other with a closeness which comes to near-identity. Thus actions which affected the social body reacted back on the physical body."[9] In ritual practice, as Mervyn James explains, the results of the social body upon the physical body include "physical ailments, for example, being seen as the result of sins, lapses or crimes which had inflicted harm on the social body."[10] The ritual process can have such impact on the person. In media the physical body is inflicted by the represented nature of the unobtainable virtual standard found in the body of media.

It is important that the relationship between the body of media and the subject-media process be understood. The body of media is the whole body of people (or the masses themselves) affected by media, and in addition, the way in which a corporeal

8. Beech, "Liminality and the Practices of Identity Reconstruction," 3.

9. Rook, "Ritual Dimension," 6–7.

10. James, "Ritual, Drama, and Social Body," 7.

body is depicted in media and the person's subjective experience of their tactile-kinesthetic body. The body of media, in all three of its manifestations, is represented by engagement of persons in the subject-media process. The resulting body of media-ritualization is media's presentation, as the corporeal body is experienced no more, but rather the persons' bodies are experienced as virtual. So the body is always virtual, from the moment an infant realizes its own body. Being so doused in media, the young child is already exposed to media's representation of themselves in the fusion process. Therefore, through fusion the real body is known as virtual.

The body of media is much akin to the body of ritual or the social body which Christians participated in during medieval times. The procession of the eucharistic elements, the broken body and shed blood of Christ, the body of the Lord of the universe, took place to glorify how God through Christ intervened on behalf of the world of sinners. This took place as Christian worship. James expresses the use of ritual surrounding the body of Christ as experienced in late-medieval English towns.[11] James states: "the final intention of the cult was, then, to express the social bond and to contribute to social integration."[12] This is exactly, through the body of media, the role media takes in bonding the masses into a univocal perspective on the meanings in life, through the subject-media process.

From a Lacanian point of view there is a lack that all persons have in the dynamics of being. Accordingly, this lack can never be filled, though all persons try to fill it through desire. The ritual around the body of Christ in medieval times is instructive of how important ritual is in the lives of the individual and the masses. James explains that, "Corpus Christi expresses the creative role of religious rite and ideology in urban societies, in which the alternative symbols and ties to lordship, lineage and faithfulness, available in countrysides, were lacking."[13] This mass procession established the presence of Christ in the church in such a way as to extend the

11. James, "Ritual, Drama, and Social Body," 4.
12. James, "Ritual, Drama, and Social Body," 4.
13. James, "Ritual, Drama, and Social Body," 4.

meaning of the church being the body of Christ. This leads one to understand the nature of media and their influence in the realm of meaning-making. Media supplant ritual to the extent that they make new meaning for the person who might otherwise find meaning in ritual. In this respect it is important to understand the body of media is taken as the individual's body as well as the body of the masses—that which makes up all the people in a society. The emaciated body of media is represented as the ideal and symbolic partitioning of the individual's psyche from the body of real experience. In this manner the person comes to understand the body of media to be sleek and slender; this is the norm created by media ritual. The screen is given procession and allegiance as the masses suffer under its sway. Each person delights with the notion of participating with the body they see on the screen.

Catherine Bell states the "complex reciprocal interaction of the body and its environment is harder to see in those classic examples of ritual where the emphasis on tradition and the enactment of codified or standardized actions lead us to take so much for granted about the way people actually do things when they are acting ritually."[14] The rite of the Corpus Christi procession ritual makes starkly apparent the participants' involvement within the body of Christ, or the magisterial body, or even the community's body. Bell is correct in that much ritual activation is taken for granted; in fact ritual was supplanted by the joy of the occasion for the individual to the greatest extent, especially through ecstatic bodily experiences.

As for the social experience of ecstasy, the masses experienced the very nature of God in the ritual of the Corpus Christi, which delineated the structure of the holy body of Christ. James explains, "The symbol was the mass, which both affirmed and created social body, which was the Body of Christ" and that the Corpus Christi procession provided a visual form of structure that secured a need for the development of "social wholeness."[15] James writes about how "liturgical formulas projected themselves into secular usage"

14. Bell, *Ritual*, 139.
15. James, "Ritual, Drama, and Social Body," 9.

to provide structure for societal systems.[16] These usages were the worldly versions of Christian expression of social structure.

The church witnessed theatrical performances go in and out of fashion. Yet by AD 925, the church found a message could be successfully conveyed theatrically. Cycles of theatrical performance throughout the year were given in the towns so as to focus the magistracy on a structure only the church could provide. In the late-medieval English townships where the Corpus Christi ritual procession was used, as James would have it, "a routine of entertainment and conviviality therefore established itself in connection with the presentation of the cycles which helped to extend and confirm the network of contacts with those whose wealth and power made them significant in the external relationships of the community."[17] The network connected each village to wealth and power.

In the posttruth world Christianity has been socially and philosophically deconstructed. The texts of the Western traditions have been demythologized, and higher critical methods have aided in these affairs. Today, media-based Christianity is characterized by networks of power and wealth; media for the church is theatrical, with large screens, and it can be a big business. Moving into the world outside the church, the bond between the wealthy elite and the entertainment industry becomes evident. The internet allows many to follow stars, celebrities, and other powerful people—that is, people with an internet presence. Media provides an essential, vital, yet generic bond without which there would be no connection for the masses, and no world village.

In this media-driven age, becoming a member of a church can mean joining an online group with an app or creating a username (anonymously, if the person wishes) or joining in the designing of a website. Sending one's email address and contact information is all it takes for one to become a member of an internet presence or organization. On the internet, hits and likes are what validates the user's feelings and makes the user socially accepted. Social acceptance is at the heart of what it is to be a part of a group of caring

16. James, "Ritual, Drama, and Social Body," 10.
17. James, "Ritual, Drama, and Social Body," 12.

people. In order to become catechized into an internet presence, or taught to be a web-based-Christian, participation in the media process of joining the church is necessary. Joining the church is a ritual matter and a media event.

The replacement of ritual by media has tremendous implications for what is lacking in the life of the person and the world. Fusion and the subject-media process have altered the world to an extent the person and masses do not realize because they are now, and have been, swimming in media from day one of the mass media era. For the most part everyone in the West has had ritual media in their life. These media representations do not entice the tactile-kinesthetic body, but they make ineluctable to the eyes and ears the experiences of a lifetime which are really not experienced at all. From virtual church rituals to everyday practices like video gaming exercise, using PCs to shop for homes, using smart phones to navigate to the virtual arenas (cinemas), watching television day in and day out, leaving the screen on at all times, checking email, taking selfies, video conferencing, checking one's phone for notifications, texting, sexting, finding dates, ordering food at the virtual kiosks, ordering coffee or dinner, shopping online, curbside pickups, internet searches for online counselors, online ordination, online education (without classroom interaction)—these media rituals have been pervasive in many lives. Therefore, it follows that media usage has results, via smart devices calculating our every slothful movement to demonstrate the benefits of the virtual, just as ritual results shaped the person and masses. Media participation has drawn many away from communion or relationship with each other within the context of a ritual realm. In the grand scheme of things ritual has been replaced by media.

# 12

# Prophesy of the Rite

THE MASSES DO NOT realize how depraved the subjective body has become, robotically connected to the media machine of the screen. The subjective body is the person's conceptual and existential experience of their body, but due to media influence and advancement, this type of bodily experience has been altered forever. Living is an experience of the body, though many do not realize the implications of this, or its meaning. Surely it is the blind being led, a pure manipulation of the body; something may hurt, but one in virtuality has no association to the pain. Persons believe living with the body is living with a thing to be manipulated. In fact, the only body one lives with is the virtual body. To live with awareness and loss in the somatic (physical) body would require an attentiveness that exists outside of any influence of media. It would be a pure physical occurrence, an experience of nature in the actual world, outside of all virtual or media devices. Sadly though, this is impossible; as it has been noted, the masses swim in media and the body experienced is the body of media.

When listening to the primal voice over the compulsions ingrained in experience by media, one is closer to the truth of bare experience of the somatic physical body. Slaves to media break the shackles and reduce its return by not entertaining doubt in the real somatic experience of their bodies. But this can only be done by not participating in media at all, and in this age it is impossible to break the chains of media. To make such a transcendental move from screen to nature would be monumental and outrageous. If successful, one would fast and cleanse the psyche, the subject of the conscious and unconscious, through a process that would be psychically and physically painful. Awareness is the key to genuine experience on the earth, firmly grounded and not grasping any fickle notion that may come one's way. Notions from the body of media scrutinized are the ones due serious consideration. But the escape from media influence is not an option. Securing an experience of the body physical will always be fickle, due to the nature of the process and relationship of the body of media. Media's obsessive emphasis on the body would turn back on itself if truth could be awakened.

To be aware would be to tell of the virtual, of the detriment to the somatic body, which media exploit. The phenomenon of bodily knowledge that shifts from everyday consciousness to the body of media and back to the body of real experience is essential for those who wish to abstain from media in daily life; again, this is only speculation, due to the body and mind being captured at even a young age. A clean cut from media involvement is probably the most difficult thing a person might try to do in the modern and postmodern world. To take on a worldview that contrasts with the body of media means total abstinence and ultimate will-power. The will to power, the existential exit from the fusion process, is the most difficult individuating process one could ever attempt. Throwing off the psychological shackles and gaining freedom from media and the fusion process is not simply discontinuing the use of media, but the deliberate refusal to be exposed to any media. This countercultural shift in personal focus has no existential equivalent to anything one has experienced. Once one is the body of media, one is fused to a process that is unceasingly engaging and unrelentingly powerful.

Why one goes on paining bodies with media's strategies, rather than listening to the signals from real bodies, is unmistakably obvious. To do otherwise is death of the virtual body, hence death indeed. Recognizing the flashes of fancy and the wrinkle-free body of media as the problem, not the solution, would be a move toward freedom. Since the body has collapsed into the body of media and lost itself in its attendant media apparatus flows, it is sure to be manipulated and many or all products will be tested on it. No longer is dialectic reasonable or possible, but the flood of simulation and stimulation provided by the screen covers the person's body and eliminates tactile experience. Media are not seeing the subject everywhere, in a totalitarian sense, but the subject follows media to every corner. The body of media creeps through consciousness, leaving mines that will ignite into full-blown obsessions within persons. In circles and cycles, one takes on a brand-name, brand-new form at every glittering moment.

The body of media as the collective understanding of the body—the body of media as that phenomenon which determines the perception of the body narrowly and broadly—involves three aspects of experience. The first aspect initiates the way subjective experiences of bodies have been hijacked by media, making evident that the concept of the somatic is altered. It is subjectivity that informs the understanding of the body, and the subject is fused to media. The second aspect is specific to the representation of bodies within media space, that is, on the screen. The third and most horrific aspect is the way it affects the masses. This aspect demonstrates the collective way the body is experienced. It does so in such a way as to eliminate any person's criteria for existence. The collective experience determines a perception of the body for each individual; nothing escapes the power of the body of media.

The postmodern philosophies of Deleuze and Baudrillard have emphasized the subject and the coming of globalization and have brought about an understanding of the interconnectivity and unity of disparate subjects. The body of media is this collective, organic and robotic, mind and machine. This body is a collection of minds both ruled by the illusion of independence and swayed by fantasy. The overbearing stream of content, meant only for consumption and only for the masses, has soared out of control. It has titillations for the body and the mind of the consumer, which are the actual body of media itself. The consumer, which is body-oriented, keeps close track of fashions and trends as they are marketed at a blistering speed, those flashes which light up the screen as it is religiously followed. Each flash leaves a trail of hunger in the throats of those who are assimilated into the grossly obscene body of media.

The masses, driven by the flashes and felicities of media, sustain a system of virtual signs which create meaning. The body of media is the extension of virtual experience of the infallible world created by media. The person meets the body of media and is seduced, with each moment, into the trap so much so that the body looks and behaves as the body of media. Therefore, the body of media then carries another property, which is the expectation of what the subjective body is supposed to be or the fashion (shape and dimensions) of the person's body in particular. It seems one must abandon, relinquish, and abstain from the sensing body and join in attunement with the body of media in order to remain sane. The body of media takes persons out of one world and distracts the person from any connection with any world. Reality can be explained via the body of media, even when such reality has not been experienced existentially. Persons aware of how the body of media affects their own perception of somatic experience can still be overwhelmed by messages that drown out any other thought.

Persons are the images that are seen, insofar as they have expectations of themselves that exceed them to the extent media drives them. The images that drive the masses are unified in media and destroy any possible dialectic. Baudrillard states: "the finest chimerical assemblage remains the coupling of thought with its exact computer replica in artificial intelligence—playing with the demarcation line between the human and the inhuman in the order of thought, and representing a mockery of thought . . ."[1] As Baudrillard speaks of artificial intelligence blurring a line, so too is the line that separates us as subjects from media also blurred in the *fusion* process.

The basic platform of the self is shifted in such a way as to alter one's perception to include it in media and interaction with violence and violation. One's very instincts are manipulated and the person that one is becomes the perfect mate for media. The two are one in process: the marriage of violation. The *formation of the*

1. Baudrillard, *Impossible Exchange*, 146.

*world*, both in singularity and as global, takes place only as media participate with the subject and vice versa. This process of participation is particularly a violation of the will of the masses. Again, with the subject-media process, there is no one to stand up against this process, which becomes a global phenomenon.

# Conclusion

IN CONCLUSION, ONE MUST ask: Is there an antidote for the disease of the subject-media process? For a certain group to come out and confront this problem would require a champion of ideals that could bring forth ritual and share ritual with the world in such a way as to obliterate the function of that process that has stolen ritual. Fusion has stolen souls and condemned individuals to a life of meaninglessness, so there must be something for the person to replace fusion with: a strong force that supersedes all of media creation. This can be found in the tradition of the rituals found in the church and its sacraments. As it stands, the body of media, the subjective experience of the body through media process, and the representation of the body in media, are the very existence of the Westerner and perhaps those in other parts of the world. There is no escaping it, no unraveling the knots that are binding the individual psyche, and indeed those of the masses. Fusion, the subject-media process, captures and violates, giving way to destitution. Arriving at this conclusion is not a stretch of the imagination; examples abound of those who are captured and enamored by the sensationalism of disease and false beauty. From the barrage of video on 9/11 to the falsities of daytime and primetime bodies, there is no way to avoid the violating nature of media. The time has come for the recognition of this matter by those who deny it; the time has come for those who know it to acknowledge it and speak into the wilderness. Lone voices that could be heard from this world are a far cry from what would be needed to defeat the univocal. There must be an institution that will become strong enough to guard its young and innocent ones from the barrage of media infiltration and devastation toward minds that might stand a chance to escape the grip of fusion. Even the most diligent family or community working toward this end experiences some form of infiltration by media. It might be a type of death to separate, but one worth finding life in.

From the postmodern indoctrination in colleges, universities, graduate schools, and seminaries came the deconstructionism known all too well to the educated today. This same word, "deconstruction," has become part of common parlance. The question is: How does such a term of flimsy definition and flexible uses and misuses become so perpetuated? It seems most likely that the media produced the perpetuation, as well as the institution of higher education through the humanities and through multimodal digital humanities. What is present in the institution of learning is the ability to unlearn and dismantle any glimmer of hope in the beauty and poetic voice outside the common strand that runs throughout and holds the deconstructionist movement together. The lifeblood of this thread is the adaptation of relativism, from science to the humanities. Through clever thought one idea became the backbone of the humanities and created a posttruth world. Jean-François Lyotard was known for his work on the "postmodern condition," as evidenced by his erudite knowledge on the state of affairs. As Lyotard explains, "It is fair to say that for the last forty years the 'leading' sciences and technologies have had to do with language" and the interpretation of it or lack of ability to do so.[1] Lyotard explains that language has become "computer language." For Lyotard, "knowledge is and will be produced in order to be sold, it is and will be consumed in order to be valorized in a new production: in both cases, the goal is exchange. Knowledge ceases to be an end in itself; it loses its 'use-value.'"[2] Just as one could imagine, media have taken hold here with precision, gaining a hierarchy and stratification of levels of meaning and decision on this front. As Lyotard explains, "knowledge in the form of an informational commodity

1. Lyotard, *Postmodern Condition*, 1.
2. Lyotard, *Postmodern Condition*, 2.

indispensable to productive power is already, and will continue to be, a major—perhaps the major—stake in the worldwide competition for power."[3] The postmodern condition arose with the application of Marxist dialectical ideation on social relationships, for example, and led to the dilemma that currently occupies the West (with the exception of the problem of the postcolonial, which challenges Western ideals, ideas, and knowledge, but cannot be addressed respectfully here).

Ben Agger explains that Herbert Marcuse "does not vitiate the basic Marx but only further develops Marx's analysis of the determinative effect of ideology and consciousness on material social relations."[4] The fusion process and the subject-media process do away with the dialectic, as explained earlier, by having only one voice. However, in understanding the argumentation that led up to deconstructionism (of which the surface will only be scratched here) other scholars are involved; Agger touches on one: Jürgen Habermas. Agger states that "Habermas, however, rejects Marx's model . . . He believes that Marx did not provide for the function of consciousness in readying revolutionary agents for political practice, indeed, that Marx reduced consciousness to an epiphenomenon automatically springing from economic relations."[5] It has been sustained here, about fusion and the univocal, that the dialectic of said Marxism has been obliterated in a way that sends it to its demise. There can be no position outside of the univocal because there is one voice expressing a multitude of aspects of the posttruth, digitized reality found solely in media and their reproduction of knowledge and reality. Therefore, just as one gets underway to argue with Marcuse and Habermas, the problem of the univocal rears its head. How can one speak intelligibly about the nature of knowledge and arguments about its construction or deconstruction while there are not two sides to the argument? In a media age, to destroy knowledge and build it back up again is the function of the sole voice crying, not in a wilderness, but rather in your face.

3. Lyotard, *Postmodern Condition*, 3.

4. Agger, "Marcuse & Habermas," 160.

5. Agger, "Marcuse & Habermas," 161.

This is the place where the Christian person finds themselves, in the wake of being scoured faceless by the cries and taunts through media devices. There is no room for dialectic, much less discussion of spiritual matters. As seen above, there is in critical thought discussion of consciousness. Going on consciousness, one may remember the consciousness razing of the new positions in the mid-to-late twentieth century, such as feminism, women's studies, and others. This is the kind of awareness an institution must be awakened to in the twenty-first century. This institution is the church; only it can reach the level of Spirit to sustain an attack from media because it is the body of Christ. The problem is Christians are so taken in by media (of all kinds), including social media, website design, television, and movies, and the like. The challenge is to break free of this engagement with media.

One might consider the following first. A few years back there arose the idea of reinventing St. Benedict, crafting his way of life in a twenty-first-century framework; consider living in a contra-cultural environment, in a monastic community-like situation cloistered around medieval church ritual. What this would look like and how it would work for Christians is demonstrated by Rod Dreher in his book *The Benedict Option: A Strategy for Christians in a Post-Christian Nation*. Now there are several post-Christian approaches for the community of faith. Life opposed to fusion would be very distinct and practicable once one escapes media presence. Such a life, in all likelihood, would look like a domestic monastery. One option a person may consider, according to Dreher, would mean

> maintaining regular times of family prayer. That means regular readings of scripture and stories from the lives of the saints—Christian heroes and heroines from ages past. 'Christian kids need Christian heroes,' says Marco Sermarini, a lay Catholic community leader in Italy. 'They need to know that following Jesus radically is not an impossible dream.' Living in a domestic monastery also means putting the life of the church first, even if you have to keep your kid out of a sports program that schedules games during your church's worship services. Even more importantly, your kids need to see you and your

spouse sacrificing attendance at events if they conflict with church. And they need to see that you are serious about the spiritual life.[6]

Another consideration would be confronting media with another power, a greater power. The zeitgeist of the church in the twentieth and twenty-first centuries has had an uphill battle against the Sisyphus-like boulders known as deconstructionism and demythologizing.

Something of substance must address such emptying philosophy and method. The church has lost its substance (the body of Christ is substance). When finding Christ in the tangible things of his body and blood, this would be a step in breaking away from the body of media. There is no dialectic involved here, but rather a replacement of one by the Other. That Other is sheer communion with Christ, in the host or the unleavened bread and the wine, the cup of redemption. David Brickner illustrates it in the following: "The Passover cup is one of the central symbols of this holiday known as the Feast of Redemption. Yet the original Passover story makes no mention whatsoever of a cup."[7] Instead, it is important to remember Jesus did use a cup during the Seder meal, on the night of his crucifixion. Brickner continues by stating Jesus had "raised a cup at least twice during the meal to make important statements about Himself."[8] Furthermore, according to Brickner, and many other scholars, "The cup of redemption stood for more than the Hebrews' escape from Egypt; it stood for the plan and purpose of God for all the ages. Judgment and salvation, wrath and redemption, are brought together in the mystery of one cup."[9] The bread is the element that will be and is the focus of Jesus Christ because it represents his body. This is the body of Jesus, which has the absolute power to break the power of the body of media. This bread is his body and does more than represent Jesus' brokenness; it has the

---

6. Dreher, *Benedict Option*, 125.
7. Brickner, "Mystery of the Passover Cup," 1.
8. Brickner, "Mystery of the Passover Cup," 1.
9. Brickner, "Mystery of the Passover Cup," 2.

power to save all from the power of the body of media and that body's allure to seduce and violate.

On the night in which he was to be betrayed, Jesus Christ met with his disciples, and he took bread, gave thanks and broke *it*, and gave *it* to them, saying, "This is My body which is broken for you; as often as you meet, do this, remembering Me" (Luke 22:19). Jesus spoke this to his disciples in regards to communion with him. One partakes in communion with God through this *ritual* which is embedded in Christian tradition from that point on as the way to access his presence. This is not the first reference to bread in Scripture, but it is the first time the Lord refers to bread being his body. This element of communion is what brings about the importance of the way Jesus' body is central to Christian ritual and doctrine. Whether it is referred to as part of communion or sacrament, the body broken is the way of entry into the death and resurrection of Jesus. The apostle Paul extended the notion of the body further in relation to communion between God and the Christian in metaphorical use. Paul referred to the church as the body of Christ. Paul stated, "Now you are Christ's body, and individually members of it" (1 Cor 12:27). Paul explains that each part has its function and characteristics or talents to offer God. This is quite unlike the body of media, which expresses one voice amidst the illusion of a multiplicity of choices; the person is left hearing in the univocal only one option. The univocal nature of the body of media demonstrates the narcissism which embodies the individual who is fused to media.

United the church must stand, refusing to be splintered by the individualism of the present culture. Schisms have happened in church history, but regardless of the supposed necessity of these groupings, all in the true sacramental church must work together to defeat the sinful forces of media. A media-driven worship is foolishly individualistic, with each person wrapped up in the media provided. Often the signifier can bring us to a different conclusion than what is represented in Scripture, and such a signifier should be recognized for what it is: an aporia. Since the person, the victim of fusion, is so enamored and only capable of taking what media offer, the lie is taken as truth; the truth given is quite forced, violating the person as their gaze is glued to the screen. By the violation of the person, to the extent they have such apposing knowledge, by no fault of their own, they cannot recognize and give regard to another person's knowledge of God. This is why there are so many Christians who desire unity, but cannot get along with their neighbor. Christianity has one God and a church on every street corner. Theological discourse has been a dialectical process, but Christianity has fallen into the trap of no longer having discursive practices, instead gathering each on their own to find truth. Hence, the relativism of the singular Christian who yearns for more truth from media, yet only finds more emptiness. This separateness of each person is a direct result of how beholden we are to the process of media. The Christian is trapped and violated by the fusion process and most of the time is either unwilling to admit it or is not conscious of the entrapment. As a measure of experience in the world, Piotr Hoffman states: "the unmanageable violence of the other threatens me [which] alienates me from all shared practices and vocabularies . . . there is *nothing* I can deploy against the deadly threat of the other, and so the world *as a whole* breaks down for me."[10] In the posttruth world, "the skeptical attitude feeds the genuine aspect" of the very nature of existence. Hoffman goes on to define this nature as "the sense of one's total powerlessness in the face of ultimate violence."[11] This violence of existence is exacerbated and lived through media process. The body of Christ was violated and broken via crucifixion.

Some argue the brutality of the crucifixion could not happen in the will of a loving God. This understanding denies the historicity of the process of Roman crucifixion and forgets the brutality of the practices of sacrifice in many other cultures. When one knows the ritual of his sacrificial death is fulfilling all other sacrificial practices, then one better appreciates his resurrection and ascension. Besides, the nature of victory came from a place of defeat, hence, the nonviolent nature of the Messiah. So in a world unfriendly to the notion of truth, seeking truth in the guise of spirituality is quite duplicitous. But it should be kept in mind that people seek spiritual matters in order to find ways of existing in a disordered

---

10. Hoffman, *Doubt, Time, Violence*, 119 (emphasis original).

11. Hoffman, *Doubt, Time, Violence*, 119.

world. Vittorio Gallese demonstrates that "living in a complex society requires individuals to develop cognitive skills enabling them to cope with other individual actions."[12] Hence, the nature of ritual is a necessary part of lives, and the church must take back its practices in order to address the lies of media. There is a need for a change of consciousness away from being media-driven toward being body-driven. The overriding bodily experience in our present digitized culture is the body of media. Media leave us robbed of our essence as corporeal beings. One can obtain true bodily experience by becoming part of the body of Christ. Through the ancient rituals of the church, ritual is regained for the postmodern person. Society is preoccupied with countless types of media, all of which promote the body of media in one of its forms or another. The body of media represents bodily experience in an unrealistic way, whereas the brokenness of the body of Christ is explicitly realistic. Every detail of the crucifixion points to the real, true, and perfect body, which exemplifies the greatest ideal of all, freedom from our nature into his.

12. Gallese, "'Shared Manifold' Hypothesis," 33.

# Bibliography

Adorno, Theodor Wiesengrund. *The Culture Industry: Selected Essays on Mass Culture*. London: Psychology, 2001.

Agger, Ben. "Marcuse & Habermas on New Science." *Polity* 9 (1976) 158–81.

Badiou, Alain. *Deleuze: The Clamor of Being*. Translated by Louise Burchill. Minneapolis: University of Minnesota Press, 2000.

Barrett, William. *Death of the Soul: From Descartes to the Computer*. New York: Anchor, 1986.

Baudrillard, Jean. *Fatal Strategies*. Los Angeles: Semiotext(e), 1990.

———. *Impossible Exchange*. Brooklyn: Verso Trade, 2012.

———. *Screened Out*. Brooklyn: Verso, 2002.

———. *Simulacra and Simulation*. Ann Arbor: University of Michigan Press, 1994.

———. *The Spirit of Terrorism*. Translated by Chris Turner. London: Verso, 2002.

———. *The Vital Illusion*. New York: Columbia University Press, 2000.

Becker, Karin. "Media and the Ritual Process." *Media, Culture & Society* 17 (1995) 629–46.

Beech, Nic. "Liminality and the Practices of Identity Reconstruction." *Human Relations* 64 (2011) 285–302.

Bell, Catherine M. *Ritual: Perspectives and Dimensions*. New York: Oxford University Press, 1997.

Bermúdez, José Luis, et al., eds. *The Body and the Self*. Cambridge: MIT Press, 1995.

Boyer, Pascal, and Pierre Liénard. "Why Ritualized Behavior? Precaution Systems and Action Parsing in Developmental, Pathological and Cultural Rituals." *Behavioral and Brain Sciences* 29 (2006) 595–613.

Brickner, David. "The Mystery of the Passover Cup." https://jewsforjesus.org/ newsletter-mar-2002/the-mystery-of-the-passover-cup.

Couldry, Nick. "Media Rituals: Beyond Functionalism." In *Media Anthropology*, edited by Eric W. Rothenbuhler and Mihai Coman, 59–69. Thousand Oaks, CA: Sage, 2005.

# BIBLIOGRAPHY

Deleuze, Gilles. *Empiricism and Subjectivity: An Essay on Hume's Theory of Human Nature.* New York: Columbia University Press, 1991.

———. *Nietzsche and Philosophy.* New York: Columbia University Press, 2006.

Deleuze, Gilles, and Félix Guattari. *What is Philosophy?* New York: Columbia University Press, 1994.

Derrida, Jacques. "The Ends of Man." *Philosophy and Phenomenological Research* 30 (1969) 31–57.

———. *Margins of Philosophy.* Chicago: University of Chicago Press, 1982.

Dreher, Rod. *The Benedict Option: A Strategy for Christians in a Post-Christian Nation.* New York: Penguin, 2017.

Ellwood, Robert. *The Politics of Myth: A Study of C. G. Jung, Mircea Eliade, and Joseph Campbell.* Albany: SUNY Press, 1999.

Evans, Dylan. *An Introductory Dictionary of Lacanian Psychoanalysis.* New York: Routledge, 1996.

Gallese, Vittorio. "The 'Shared Manifold' Hypothesis. From Mirror Neurons to Empathy." *Journal of Consciousness Studies* 8 (2001) 33–50.

Glowinski, Huguette, et al., eds. *A Compendium of Lacanian Terms.* London: Free Association, 2001.

Gurevitch, Zali, and Gideon Aran. "Never in Place: Eliade and Judaic Sacred Space." *Archives de Sciences Sociales des Religions* (1994) 135–52.

Hanisch, Carol. "The Personal is Political." https://webhome.cs.uvic. ca/~mserra/AttachedFiles/PersonalPolitical.pdf.

Hoffman, Piotr. *Doubt, Time, Violence.* Chicago: University of Chicago Press, 1986.

James, Mervyn. "Ritual, Drama and Social Body in the Late Medieval English Town." *Past & Present* 98 (1983) 3–29.

Johnson, Dru. *Human Rites: The Power of Rituals, Habits, and Sacraments.* Grand Rapids: Eerdmans, 2019.

Johnston, Adrian. "Jacques Lacan." (2013). In *Stanford Encyclopedia of Philosophy,* edited by Edward N. Zalta. https://plato.stanford.edu/entries/lacan/.

Kapferer, Bruce. "Ritual Dynamics and Virtual Practice: Beyond Representation and Meaning." *Social Analysis* 48 (2004) 33–54.

Konvalinka, Ivana, et al. "Synchronized Arousal between Performers and Related Spectators in a Fire-Walking Ritual." *Proceedings of the National Academy of Sciences* 108 (2011) 8514–19.

Lacan, Jacques. *The Four Fundamental Concepts of Psychoanalysis.* New York: Routledge, 2018.

———. "Of Structure as an Inmixing of an Otherness Prerequisite to Any Subject Whatever." *The Languages of Criticism and the Sciences of Man* (1970) 186–200.

———. "The Seminar of Jacques Lacan: Book XIII: The Object of Psychoanalysis: 1965–1966." Unpublished lecture. Translated by Cormac Gallagher. 2011. http://hdl.handle.net/10788/162.

Lacan, Jacques, and Bruce Fink. *Ecrits: A Selection.* New York: Norton, 2002.

Lawson, Hilary. *Reflexivity: The Post-Modern Predicament.* Essex, UK: Hutchinson, 1985.

Leder, Drew. *The Absent Body.* Chicago: University of Chicago Press, 1990.

Lyotard, Jean-François. *The Postmodern Condition: A Report on Knowledge.* Cambridge History of Literary Criticism 10. Minneapolis: University of Minnesota Press, 1984.

Massumi, Brian. "Realer than Real." *Copyright* 1 (1987) 90–97.

Montgomery, Kathryn C. *Generation Digital: Politics, Commerce, and Childhood in the Age of the Internet.* Cambridge: MIT Press, 2009.

Murphy, Shane M. "A Social Meaning Framework for Research on Participation in Social Online Games." *Journal of Media Psychology* 12 (2007) 1–33.

Pauly, John. "Ritual Theory and the Media." In *The Handbook of Media and Mass Communication Theory,* edited by Robert S. Fortner and Mark Fackler, 172–89. West Sussex, UK: Wiley & Sons, 2014.

Pavlina, Steve. *Personal Development for Smart People.* Carlsbad, CA: Hay House, 2008.

Peltz, Jennifer. "To Some Psychiatric Patients, Life Seems Like TV." https://www.foxnews.com/printer_friendly_wires/2008Nov24/0,4675,TrumanSyndrome,oo.html.

Rodriguez, Silvia. "Subject." In *A Compendium of Lacanian Terms,* edited by Hughette Glowinski et al., 192–97. New York: Free Association, 2001.

Rook, Dennis W. "The Ritual Dimension of Consumer Behavior." *Journal of Consumer Research* 12 (1985) 251–64.

Rorty, Richard. *Irony, Contingency, and Solidarity.* Cambridge: Cambridge University Press, 1989.

Sacks, Oliver. *The Man Who Mistook His Wife for a Hat.* New York: Touchstone, 1998.

Sacks, Peter. *Generation X Goes to College. An Eye-Opening Account of Teaching in Postmodern America.* Chicago: Open Court, 1996.

Sen, Biswarup. "Information as Ritual: James Carey in the Digital Age." *Cultural Studies ↔ Critical Methodologies* 17 (2017) 473–81.

Sheets-Johnstone, Maxine. *The Roots of Power: Animate Form and Gendered Bodies.* Chicago: Open Court, 1994.

Shumway, David R. *Michel Foucault.* 1989. Reprint, Charlottesville: University Press of Virginia, 1992.

Silverman, Kaja. *The Subject of Semiotics.* New York: Oxford University Press, 1983.

Smith, James K. A. *You Are What You Love: The Spiritual Power of Habit.* Grand Rapids: Brazos, 2016.

Stout, Martha. *The Myth of Sanity: Divided Consciousness and the Promise of Awareness.* New York: Penguin, 2002.

Szakolczai, Arpad. "Liminality and Experience: Structuring Transitory Situations and Transformative Events." *International Political Anthropology* 2 (2009) 141–72.

Ulam, Stanislaw M. *Adventures of a Mathematician.* Berkeley: University of California Press, 1991.

Verhaeghe, Paul. "Causation and Destitution of a Pre-Ontological Non-Entity: On the Lacanian Subject." In *Key Concepts of Lacanian Psychoanalysis,* edited by Dany Nobus, 164–89. New York: Routledge, 2018.

Watzlawick, Paul, ed. *The Invented Reality: How Do We Know What We Believe We Know?: Contributions to Constructivism.* New York: Norton, 1984.

Wegner, Daniel M. *White Bears and Other Unwanted Thoughts: Suppression, Obsession, and the Psychology of Mental Control.* New York: Penguin, 1989.

Žižek, Slavoj. *The Fragile Absolute: Or, Why Is the Christian Legacy Worth Fighting For?* Brooklyn: Verso, 2001.

———. *How to Read Lacan.* London: Granta, 2011.

———. *Organs Without Bodies: On Deleuze and Consequences.* London: Routledge, 2004.

———. *Tarrying With the Negative: Kant, Hegel, and the Critique of Ideology.* Durham, NC: Duke University Press, 1993.